Client Sci

The Five Cs Marketing Plan for Professionals

Rachel Killeen

Chartered Accountants Ireland

Published by
Chartered Accountants Ireland
Chartered Accountants House
47-49 Pearse Street
Dublin 2
www.charteredaccountants.ie

This publication is designed to provide accurate and authoritative information in regard to the subject matter covered. It is provided on the understanding that The Institute of Chartered Accountants in Ireland is not engaged in rendering professional services. If professional advice or other expert assistance is required, the services of a competent professional should be sought.

ISBN 978-0-903854-93-1

Typeset by Typeform
Printed by ColourBooks

To
Sheila Killeen
and
Michael Torpey

CONTENTS

Part IV: Collaborate

Part V: Calculate

Appendix

Acknowledgements

I owe an enormous debt of gratitude to all those people who helped me to put this book together – especially the fifty-five professionals (who are named in the Appendix) for their time, their inspiration and their insights into their highly professional practices.

Thank you to Michael Diviney, editor, publisher and mentor, for his unwavering encouragement and excellent clarity. Angela Carr, Clare Loughnane and Emmanuel Ranchin gave their valuable time challenging and proofreading, and that is so much appreciated. Ted Corcoran is truly inspirational. Ana Nelson is incredibly knowledgeable. Padhraig Nolan's design skills and advice are second to none.

Thanks also to three great people, Russell Carlson, Bill Sullivan and Sheila Sullivan, who were there from the beginning.

Client: noun a person using the services of a professional person or organisation.

Science (from the Latin *scientia*, from *scire* 'know'). The intellectual and practical activity encompassing the systematic study of the structure and behaviour of the physical and natural world through observation and experiment. **2** a systematically organised body of knowledge on any subject.

Source: The Oxford English Dictionary

Introduction

'These are days when many are discouraged. In the ninety-three years of my life, depressions have come and gone. Prosperity has always returned and will again.'

John D. Rockefeller

Client Science is written specifically for those who want to grow their practice. You may be an accountant, an architect, a banker, a broker, a doctor, an engineer, an IT consultant, a photographer, a solicitor or a zoologist. If you want to attract more clients, then **Client Science** is for you. This book tells you, in five practical steps, how to create a marketing plan that will help you to find new markets, satisfy your clients and garner a more profitable and successful reputation in the marketplace.

The best professionals make the smartest choices. They carefully decide what types of clients they want to attract, the range of services they will provide, and the best media to use to promote their practice. The aim of this book is to present you with practical ideas, or '**Applied Science**', so that you can take advantage of new opportunities and attract more clients.

I started writing **Client Science** just before the global economy started to slow down. I had recently left banking after twenty years in marketing, client relations and business development. My work involved marketing to professional, SME, corporate, and capital markets clients of the bank. Competition was intense in the sector. If we did not meet the needs of our clients, there was always another bank waiting to take our place.

Some would say that I chose the right time to leave banking, even though I could not have foreseen the future. As the world's economic crisis began, I was travelling in South-east Asia: visiting hill tribes along the Mekong river, bartering at the markets in Laos, and sharing tea and ideas with the old ladies and gents of Dong village in Guangxi province in China. There was a serious aspect to my travels, however. It was a fact-finding mission. I wanted to learn about Eastern business culture.

Travelling through Asia taught me five important lessons:

Anything is possible. You can run a bustling business selling mangos on a railway track under a bridge. You can produce incredible food for a group of tourists by sowing a small patch of land, keeping chickens, and using a wok. You can carry a family of five as well as the contents of a market stall on a moped. Grandmother on the seat, the two-year-old wearing the helmet, father carrying the fruit, mother holding the umbrella, and the ten-year-old steering the moped through the narrow streets.

Genuine relationships are vital. You cannot help but feel a genuine connection with the people you meet in Asia. Although we did not speak the same language, memorable relationships were formed out of our common interest in learning about each other: how we were different, how we were similar, what our cultures were all about. Business thrives on real relationships.

Be prepared to bargain. Business is about making a deal that represents good value for each of the parties involved. A good business relationship should flow naturally between people and it is most successful when there is great service, clear feedback, continuous improvement, and sufficient money involved to cover costs, as well as some profit. In Laos, bargaining was fierce and great fun. The vendors knew their limits and the aim was always to get a win–win result.

Think differently. In a saturated market – and few markets are as competitive as those in Asia – you have to be prepared to be innovative to succeed. In some of the towns I visited, it came down to our basic human needs. Success was the difference between eating or not eating.

Do what you are good at. It is almost impossible to excel unless you are deeply interested in and committed to what you do. Identify your strengths and those of your team, and use those skills to win more clients. The food we ate in the tribal villages of Vietnam was better than any I had ever tasted. It was cooked with immense skill in the most basic cooking facilities, from the freshest ingredients, and with an impressive level of perfectionism.

Client Science began with business lessons learned while travelling from Hanoi to Hong Kong. Shortly after I started writing the book, the economy deteriorated significantly and a global crisis was declared. When I returned to Ireland, I spent a considerable amount of time meeting with and talking to professional people about their concerns, their business development efforts and the challenges they faced in their practices at a time of recession. I interviewed fifty-five people for the book: their names and the practices and firms they work with are listed in the **Appendix**. Many of the observations made by the people I spoke to are confidential to their particular practice or organisation. For this reason, in my case studies (or '**Test Cases**') and references, I describe the people that I interviewed only by the profession they practice: accountant, architect, banker, consultant or solicitor, for example.

Here are the top five concerns expressed by the professionals I spoke to:

A shrinking pool of new clients

'New clients used to just arrive on our doorstep, referred on by our other clients. We could barely keep up with the demand. Now it has all dried up.'

Photographer

Not getting paid

'Many of our clients just can't afford to pay us for work we have done. That means we have to make people redundant, because we can't afford to pay them.'

Solicitor

Not generating sufficient fees

'People just want something for nothing. They get you to draw out the plans, give them ideas, make recommendations, and they want you to cut your fees by 50 percent – which makes the work unprofitable. We can't sustain that long-term.'

Architect

Clients no longer availing of services

'Our top three clients won't even make it into the top ten next year. How do we replace them? That is our greatest challenge.'

Lawyer

No marketing experience

'We have never had to do marketing. We know we have to, to attract new clients. Where do we start?'

Accountant

My aim in writing this book was to provide a useful marketing guide, to help you drive the profitability of your business and practice. I am conscious that some professionals have an uncomfortable impression of aspects of marketing, such as aggressive advertising, cold-calling and unsolicited mail. This is not the type of marketing I advocate. The reality is that most successful professionals use a sophisticated level of marketing. Even President Barack Obama could not have been elected without a skilled marketing team engaged to help him communicate his policies and values.

In setting priorities for marketing, it is important to reflect briefly on what the term 'marketing' actually means. The standard industry definition of marketing is: 'to satisfy clients' needs at a profit'.

In a time of plenty, we can become complacent about how we meet clients' needs, and we often focus more on the profitability aspect of the relationship. We do our best, of course, but because we are dealing with high demand it is hard to find time to be ultra-creative, to give clients outstanding service, or to consider how we will add new facets to our business for the future. When times are good, we work so hard to keep up that the future just happens.

In a time of scarcity, there is more time to consider your business interests, your clients and your future. That is what I am asking you to do here. You want your clients to come back for more; to recommend you to others; to consider you above your competitors. **Client Science** is designed to help you formulate a marketing plan to attract and retain more clients.

How to use this book

You may already have a formal, written marketing plan or you may not. In researching this book, most of the sole practitioners I spoke to admitted that they have no marketing plan whatsoever. Relatively few of the people that I encountered believe that their marketing plan is adequately structured to help them build their practice.

Client Science is designed so that you can put together a marketing plan to win in five clear steps:

I.   Collate,

II. Create,

III. Communicate,

IV. Collaborate and

V.   Calculate.

These are the 'Five Cs' for your marketing plan. Each chapter of the book contains practical information to help you to develop your plan. Wherever possible, I have included:

- marketing and innovation theory ('**Science Theory**'),

- hard facts ('**Science Facts**'),

- case studies ('**Test Cases**'),

- amusing and true stories ('**Science Fiction**'),

- plus useful examples and practical ideas for the implementation of your marketing plan ('**Applied Science**').

There are also '**Science Experiments**' for you to try, and quotes from the marketing profession's '**Top Scientists**' to reflect on. (**Figure 1** on page 7 shows you how the book is structured).

Many of the marketing plans I reviewed as part of my research included background information about the business environment, but they did not necessarily describe how to innovate, communicate, forge relationships or measure the results of marketing initiatives. **Client Science** describes how to take your marketing planning beyond the research stage to implementation. Most of the practitioners I spoke to were highly successful for the following two reasons:

- **They plan.** Each of these winning teams uses regular and flexible planning to ensure that their capabilities are harnessed to maximum effect.

- **They innovate.** They use their strengths to create a service proposition that truly impresses their target clients.

How do you formulate a marketing plan that will help you stand out from the crowd and that will drive you to a more profitable future? Whatever success means to you, it is possible to formulate a plan that will get you there. Planning for business success need not be overly complicated. What you really need is a practical path to help you get the best out of your client base, your particular practice or firm, and your professional capability.

Client Science encourages you to think about all aspects of what you present to the market – in a new and interesting way. Here is a brief summary of each of the **Five Cs**:

1. The background to your practice and your market environment is important. This is covered in Part I of the plan, **Collate**, in which my aim is to help you to research your professional goals, your clients' needs, your market and your competition, so that you can make informed decisions about what you want to achieve, and then go for it.

2. To stand out, you have to be innovative. Part II of the plan helps you to **Create** a better service for your clients. What value can you offer your clients? How can you

give your clients an exceptionally positive experience? How can you differentiate what you offer from your competitors?

3. Part III of *Client Science* explains how to **Communicate**. Can you describe the unique service you offer in just one sentence? What is your 'thirty-second elevator pitch', and can everyone in your firm recite it? New technology; defining moments in client relationships; communication that goes beyond the norm: innovation in your practice will reveal itself in extraordinary ways, and yet impressive communication can be as simple as sending flowers to a client on the birth of a child.

4. Collaboration is usually the unwritten part of a marketing plan. In the current market environment, it is a good idea to formally review all your relationships with people both inside and outside your practice. People who can help you to promote your business in the local and extended community are often called 'key influencers'. Part IV, **Collaborate,** looks at how you can network with key people such as clients, colleagues, community leaders, collaborators and even competitors to get business referrals.

5. Part V of the marketing plan, and of *Client Science*, is **Calculate**. Why would you invest in marketing unless there was some way to measure the results? I outline five ways you can calculate the success of your marketing plan so that you can get real results from your campaigns.

The introduction for each part of the book has a diagram showing you how each section of the marketing plan is formulated. It is up to you to choose the sections that you believe are relevant to your practice. You can use this book as a formula for your marketing plan or read through it to get ideas – whichever suits your needs best.

Most of the people that I interviewed felt that there was no longer such a thing as 'business as usual'; this is because the market they operate in has altered significantly in the recent past. It means that they are forced by market dynamics to take a completely new approach to how they recruit new clients, how they meet and exceed clients' expectations, and how they can actually get paid for the work they do.

Client Science is not about business as usual; it is about 'business unusual'. The headings for the marketing plan are designed to help you be more innovative in an environment that presents new challenges – which are probably different from any you have experienced before. The **Five Cs – Collate, Create, Communicate, Collaborate and Calculate** – will help you to conceive new and creative ways to impress your existing clients, promote your practice, and attract new clients.

Figure 1. The Structure of *Client Science*

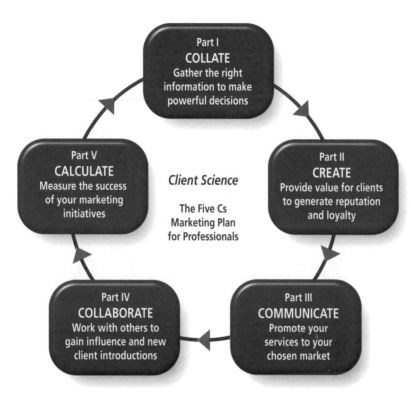

Why Five?

You may be wondering why the constant reference to the number five? In my experience of compiling plans for professional clients, each of the five elements – **Collate, Create, Communicate, Collaborate** and **Calculate** – are the five headings of a solid, well-structured marketing plan. They contain the creative thinking, the communication and the relationship angles that are of paramount importance to a professional in practice. They also incorporate the metrics, statistics and figures required to review, forecast and measure a campaign. These five headings are specifically designed to meet your needs.

Again, the concept of keeping ideas to five evolved from my interviews. I asked all those I interviewed for their opinion on what a useful marketing book would look like. People suggested that a marketing book should incorporate five main points: it should be **short, simple, useful, memorable** and **relevant**.

When it comes to brainstorming new ideas, you can come up with a hundred, but a busy practice is likely only to have time and resources to implement five at most. If you and your team manage to implement up to five new ideas from those presented in each of the chapters, then well done. If you achieve more than five, that is a superb performance.

Some misconceptions about marketing

- **'We can't afford it.'** Not true. Marketing is not just about advertisements or glossy brochures or personal selling – though these tactics play a part. Marketing is about relationship-building and about creating a client-focused culture in your practice or business. **It is about collaborating with people who can help you achieve your goals**. Modern marketing is highly cost-effective. Internet marketing can be used to reach millions of potential clients at a remarkably low cost.

- **'It's a waste of money.'** Not true. Where money is spent on relationship building, it represents an investment that is specifically made with the objective of generating income. You can also calculate the return on your investment to evaluate which methods generate the best business return.

- **'It's best to get someone else to do it.'** Not true. Marketing should be a completely integrated part of the activity of your practice or business. Marketing is everything you and your team do to address clients' needs, whether it is the transparency of the invoices you send, the quality of your website or the professionalism of your team.

Marketing is the support system that helps you to take a leadership position – in your practice, in your community and most importantly in the minds of your clients. Marketing gives you the tools to help you to identify the clients that you want to do business with, to understand their needs intimately and to ensure that you adapt your professional services to be current, relevant to the market and, above all, innovative and interesting. **Client Science** will help you to become a better leader, a better practitioner and a better communicator with the ultimate objective of becoming more successful in your professional life.

Part I   Collate

Gather the right information to make powerful decisions

1. **Set Objectives:** Agree your top five goals

2. **Practice Analysis:** Five levels of understanding

3. **Customer Relationship Management:** Five ways to find new clients

4. **Clients:** Five important client insights

5. **Competition:** High five! Be the best in the market

Set Objectives:
Agree your top five goals

*'A long habit of not thinking a thing wrong, gives it
a superficial appearance of being right'*

Thomas Paine

A challenging goal

All of the fifty-five professionals that I interviewed for this book share one common characteristic: they are passionate about clients and about the quality of service that they provide. Each professional devotes considerable time and energy to building strong relationships with clients, communicating with them and finding ways to improve their service to clients.

These practitioners tend to set objectives for their practice that are based on fulfilling the needs of their clients. It is no surprise then, that all of them are highly successful in their field.

I believe that the vast majority of professionals care about the welfare and wellbeing of their clients. However, it is difficult to create the sort of utopia that will inspire their long-term loyalty, particularly in the current market environment. You might dream about the innovative services you would provide for your clients, if you only had more time and resources, but the reality may be that your clients' experience of your practice is not as positive as you want it to be. You are not alone. Most professionals in practice have an overall vision of how they would like to service clients in a perfect world. In **Client Science**, I challenge you to persevere, focus on the objective achieve that vision.

Writing about challenge reminds me of days I spent trekking in the Vietnamese jungle. Our objective was to reach Halong Bay, which I had heard described as one of the most beautiful waterscapes in the world. The trek was tough and fraught with dangers – snakes, poisonous spiders, difficult terrain. If it weren't for the dream of Halong Bay, I would have turned back.

This experience in Vietnam taught me how important it is to work at achieving your vision. If you set clear objectives the potential for your professional practice, in terms of growth and client experience, is limitless.

The best objectives present a dream for the heart, a challenge for the head and a journey worth making the effort for. We could call these objectives: 'higher goals'.

What are objectives?

Science Theory

Objectives are clearly articulated goals or statements of intent. If you are in practice to provide a particular professional service to clients, there should be at least one statement about how you are going to improve what you offer for the benefit of your clients.

Naturally, every professional firm must find the delicate balance between delivering an outstanding service to clients, satisfying the career needs of the professional staff who are providing that service, and ensuring the financial success of the practice.[1]

A lack of client-focused objectives in a professional practice can be explained by the dynamics of the marketplace over the past decade. In boom times, many professionals concurred in not having – or needing – a formal plan for their future. They were too busy keeping up with clients' demands for their services.

Most, if not all, of them had set annual objectives or goals. These objectives were often referred to as 'targets'. They were generally an estimate of the number of new clients that could potentially be recruited over the course of the year and the forecasted level of income likely to be generated. If long hours were put in and they were prepared to deliver a good service to clients, then income streams were guaranteed to grow annually and incrementally. Planning, and in particular objective-setting, tended to be informal and flexible. Income objectives were often surpassed. Once those objectives had been delivered, employees and partners tended to be rewarded accordingly.

This dedicated focus on income targets worked for the professionals I spoke to – until it failed. It failed when clients stopped spending to the same degree that they had over the past decade, and suddenly decline in growth occurred.

The problem was that members of the firm were not rewarded on delivery of customer-oriented goals such as increased satisfaction ratings, innovation or customer loyalty. They were rewarded primarily on delivery of income targets. This created an imbalance, as both quality of service and relationship-building were sacrificed in favour of achieving new sales, new income streams and new markets.

New era, new venture, new objectives

This is a new era because of the substantially altered economic climate in which we are now operating. A high proportion of professionals in practice now have to struggle

---

1. David Maister. *Managing the Professional Services Firm* (Simon & Schuster UK Ltd, 2003)

to retain clients, to recruit new clients and to make sufficient income to remain solvent. It is time to take a much more structured approach to planning and objective setting in order to protect and build your practice for the future.

Perhaps you have to revise your CV to find a new job. Maybe you have to go out looking for new clients. Maybe you are in discussions with clients about fees. If so, my experience as a consultant working with professionals engaged in sustaining their practices suggests that you should approach objective-setting as if you were starting a new venture. The plan for last year, and the previous year, is probably not indicative of the vision you need for the coming year, or the challenges you will face. As Jack Welch said:

'When all the paraphernalia is stripped away, the leader must articulate a vision.'

Play to your strengths at every opportunity. Consider your objectives from the point of view of your clients. Think about what aspects of your service clients praise most highly; what you are best at; the roles you are passionate about. If you are clear about what you are excellent at, you will find it easier to inspire clients and to attract new clients to your practice.

How to set five intelligent and challenging objectives

Applied Science

Setting objectives begins with what you want to achieve. One of the most enlightened conversations I had in researching this book was with a financial markets expert. Here's his approach to setting objectives:

'Take a step back entirely from your day-to-day role and ask the question: what does success look like for your clients? How do you want to be perceived by your clients and prospective clients as an organisation in a year's time, two years' time, and five years' time?

Then look at where the gaps are. Think: what do you have to do to bridge those gaps and get to where you want to be so that clients will want to do business with you? Then shape the business to fill in those gaps. Some adjustments you can make immediately; others happen over time.

You'd be surprised by how quickly things come together once you choose your direction. This is a useful – in fact a liberating – exercise because it gives you permission to strip away the routine issues, the constraints and the usual tasks that are inherent in running a business. It also allows you to imagine the future of your practice as it could be, at its very best.'

Financial markets director

Once you have identified the broad direction you want to travel in, it is important to articulate clearly the objectives that will challenge you to get there. 'SMART' is a well-known acronym used to explain the elements that you have to keep in mind when setting your objectives.

Science Fact

SMART objectives are:

- **Specific**: Objectives should specify what you want to achieve.

- **Measurable**: You should be able to measure whether you are meeting the objectives or not.

- **Achievable**: Are the objectives you set achievable and attainable?

- **Realistic**: Can you realistically achieve the objectives with the resources that you have?

- **Timeframe**: Set a timeframe that states by when you will achieve your objectives.

Science Experiment

Objectives should have two additional elements: they should be exciting and rewarding. Add an 'E' and an 'R' to 'SMART' to make your objectives 'SMARTER'.

- **Exciting**: Objectives should be dynamic, heartfelt and challenging. They are designed to make people feel that they want to be part of the team that seeks to achieve those goals. Imagine the types of objectives that Richard Branson sets for Virgin.

- **Rewarding:** For most of us, that means a more profitable business, more satisfied clients and, very importantly, highly motivated employees.

Here are five types of objectives that lend balance to your organisation:

Figure 2. Set Objectives: Your Top Five Goals

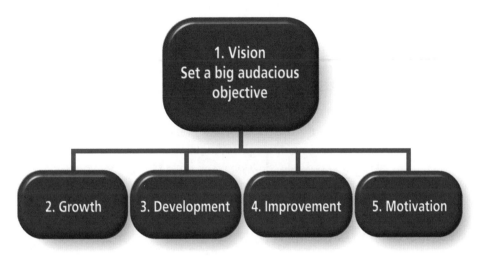

1. A vision, or a big audacious objective

Think about the long-term vision for your professional practice. Your first objective should be both inspirational and aspirational. Who, what, and where do you want to be, from a client's perspective, in six months, one year and five years? This big, audacious objective is about positioning your practice in the market against competitors and in the community. This is a dynamic objective. It should be attainable, yet highly challenging.

An example of a big, audacious objective is: 'To be the number one provider of accountancy services to entrepreneurs in the North Region by 2014, as defined by reputation and profitability.' All other objectives should support the delivery of this one.

A sole practitioner will set different objectives to those of a partnership, and so I have separated the two to discuss them in more detail:

Sole Practitioner

Perhaps you want to grow your practice into a firm and take on partners to provide a greater range of services to clients. Maybe you want to retire in five years' time. Perhaps you want to merge with another complementary firm. Or you might want to grow the practice fivefold over the next year. Maybe you see a gap in the market for a service that clients need but which you are not yet qualified to provide – and your audacious goal is to retrain and set up in practice in this new field.

I found in my research that sole practitioners were the least likely to set objectives for their business and that relatively few have marketing plans in place. My advice is to set objectives each year and to steer your practice towards those goals. Think carefully about what you need to do to achieve your big, audacious goal. Do you have to train for it, invest in it, or forge new relationships in order to achieve it?

As a sole practitioner, you might also consider how you can make space for your own professional interests in your work life. This could be the start of some seriously creative thinking: learning new skills, developing an online market for your services or simply developing a new set of contacts.

Partnership or firm

As a leader in a partnership or a firm, you have a mix of people, skill sets and experience on your team. You will probably want to engage with the other partners in the firm to decide what your big, audacious goal is. The most important thing is to get support and input into your objectives from those who can help you to achieve them. This goal is shared by all those who work in the practice.

The audacious goal – or you could call it a vision for your practice – is the one overarching goal that you want to achieve for your clients over a period of time. In my experience, teams work together far more effectively if there is one vision for the organisation. A major client-focused objective has the power to create excitement, teamwork and commitment.

Overcoming major challenges

This is a time of great change and upheaval for professionals in practice. It means that the vision for your practice may be about overcoming a fundamental challenge such as surviving and growing over the next eighteen months in a contracting market. If you ever wonder how you can possibly overcome the challenges that you encounter in managing your practice, consider the amazing accomplishments of the Irish rugby star Brian O'Driscoll.

Top Scientist

Brian O'Driscoll's eyesight has always been 30 percent of the average. As captain of the Irish rugby team, O'Driscoll led his team to win the Triple Crown, the Six Nations Championship and Ireland's first Grand Slam in sixty-one years. All of these accomplishments were achieved with one third of the normal eyesight. He postponed having an eye operation because he was concerned that if something went wrong, it might damage his career. Only in late 2009 did he have an operation to resolve the eye problem.[2] There are many professionals experiencing grave difficulties in their practice at present. When you consider the magnitude of what Brian O'Driscoll has achieved, there is nothing that you cannot overcome.

2. Growth

Income is an important objective – it may even be your big, audacious objective – but it should not be the sole objective for your practice. If income is the only objective, it becomes what I call a limiting objective. What do I mean by a limiting objective? Experience tells us that simply focusing on income has not worked because it is purely a short-term approach and, therefore, limiting.

The problem with focusing solely on income growth as an objective for business is that the business can fail due to lack of diversification. Feedback from my research indicates that practitioners did not have the time or inclination to diversify their business interests, develop new services, or seek out new types of clients or markets. Understandably, the focus for many practices was on providing service to clients according to their demands. The lesson is that you need to consciously seek out a wider portfolio of clients rather than simply focusing on those clients that turn up.

The second lesson that many professionals have learned is one of financial management. Most people simply spend more in the boom times, because they can afford to. Unfortunately, a change of attitude has been forced upon professionals as they struggle to manage high costs in a lower-revenue environment.

Set a realistic and achievable income growth and cost-management target. If your financial targets are set, then you are more likely to take the steps necessary to achieve those targets. An example of an income target is 'to increase income by 12 percent to €5 million by 2014'.

3. Development

Review your existing clients; identify the needs and requirements of the clients that you serve best; set objectives to recruit more of the clients you know you can do your best work for.

---

2. Profile of Brian O'Driscoll: 'Sporting hero on top of his game'. *Sunday Times,* 27 December 2009, Pg. 15

When times were good and there was a plentiful supply of clients, people tended to focus exclusively on the business that was easy to reach, often called 'the low-hanging fruit'. The Irish property and construction sector provided an enormous amount of business to accountants, solicitors, bankers and other professionals during that time. So much so, in fact, that some professional entities tended to ignore other opportunities, such as the international marketplace and other indigenous industries that had the potential to offer more steady income streams but were perceived as being less lucrative at the time. Those firms that sought to achieve balance across their income streams, incorporating indigenous industry, international business, construction and other sectors, attained far greater success and stability in recent times than those that focused solely on one or two fast-growth sectors.

This rule does not only apply to practitioners involved in servicing the business community. People who provide professional services to individuals experienced similar issues. While income streams were there, people focused solely on the business that walked in the door, instead of setting objectives to identify the needs of, and seek to attract, a broader, more diverse range of clients.

An example of a clients-related objective is: 'By understanding and fulfilling the accounting requirements of entrepreneurs, we will identify, target and recruit 2,000 new start-up businesses by June 2012.'

4. Improvement

Decide on the range of services that you will offer to the market. Most people gravitate towards the work they are best at. If you are good at something, or your team have particularly specialist skills, then you, and they, are more inclined to devote maximum effort to it. The problem is that as time goes by you might forget about what you particularly enjoy and find yourself drifting into other areas, simply because the work comes your way. Stand back and think again about the services that you really enjoy and excel at providing.

Applied Science

The market has changed significantly, and as a result the demand for certain types of products has fallen, whereas for other services, it has increased dramatically. Examine the market, find out what clients want, and adapt your practice to serve a wider audience.

'We're focusing more on liquidations, because there's a demand for that service in the current market environment. My team and I trained specifically to deal with liquidations over the past year.'

Partner, medium-sized accountancy firm

Reviewing your range of products and services will also include the operational aspects of those products and services. Can you provide an online version of what you offer: for example, online accounts filing or online booking for doctors' appointments, or the processing of straightforward legal documents via an internet portal?

An example of a product/service-based objective is: 'We will research, develop and pilot a low-cost online accountancy facility for new start-up entrepreneurs by June 2011.'

5. Motivation

Whether you are a sole practitioner or a partner, people are vital in helping you to achieve your goals. For a sole practitioner, your objective will focus on harnessing collaborators and influencers in the market so that they can refer potential clients on to you, wherever possible. As a partner, your employees are important in helping you to win and retain business. Choose an objective that focuses on people development, morale and teamwork, as the following example from the Beacon Private Hospital in Dublin demonstrates:

Applied Science

'Our vision is to be a beacon of excellence in Irish healthcare. We will position ourselves as the predominant healthcare provider within the community we serve. Our services will be provided by dedicated, competent and talented people focused on continuous improvement and service excellence.'[3]

The 'people' aspect of your vision is about making your vision inspirational as well as aspirational. Brian O'Driscoll was named RTÉ Sports Person of the Year in 2009 not just for his brilliance as a rugby player but also for his inspirational qualities as a captain in motivating a team of people to work together to overcome every major challenge that they encountered. Objectives on paper cannot take a practice to a successful place, but your people, your energy and your commitment can.

Overall objectives for your practice should be rooted in the personal plans for each individual working in the organisation. In addition, the needs of those individuals should be recorded in the overall objectives of the practice.

An example of a people-based objective is: 'To recognise our people who work to increase client satisfaction ratings, to introduce new clients to the practice and who come up with innovative ways to attract and retain clients.'

---

3. Ted Corcoran, *The Leadership Bus* (AuthorHouse, 2008)

Summary

A major part of the success in setting objectives is the leadership aspect; you must involve people. As James Fisher once said:

> 'Leadership is the special quality that enables people to stand up and pull the rest of us over the horizon.'[4]

Communicate your objectives to the people that can help you so that they are empowered to help you to succeed. Finally and importantly, objectives should also be exciting and dynamic, so that the path to achieving them is a crusade and not a chore. You need to challenge yourself and your team to reach an audacious, client-focused goal that leads to great rewards at the end of a focused journey.

---

4. Quoted by Ted Corcoran, *The Leadership Bus* (as above)

Practice Analysis:
Five levels of understanding

2

*'The issue is really market 'sensing' or understanding.
If you can find better ways of listening to customers,
the pay-off may be enormous.'*

Nigel Piercey, Cranfield School of Management

All of the professionals that I interviewed for this book agreed that an annual review of the business, the marketplace, clients and competitors is important. However, the big issues, such as a shrinking pool of new clients, not getting paid, and clients no longer availing of services, have to be tackled first. These pressing issues won't wait for long strategic planning sessions or reports to be signed off 'whenever'. They require action now.

This chapter takes the set of objectives that were discussed in the previous chapter and translates them into positive actions. The **five levels of understanding** about your practice is a review of the fitness of your practice to achieve your objectives. We focus on bridging gaps: the aspects of your practice that may inhibit your achievement of your big, audacious goal. We also look at how you can harness your great strengths, and how you can use the opportunities presented to you in the market to succeed. The five levels of understanding refer to what you have to do to overcome hurdles and shape your business in order to attain your objectives.

Figure 3. Practice Analysis: Five levels of understanding

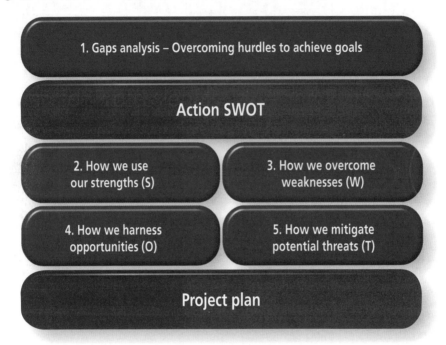

1. Gaps analysis – Overcoming hurdles to achieve goals

Action SWOT

2. How we use our strengths (S)

3. How we overcome weaknesses (W)

4. How we harness opportunities (O)

5. How we mitigate potential threats (T)

Project plan

1. Gaps analysis

First, you determine your 'desired outcome', which is where you want to be in six months, or in a year, or in five years. From that 'desired outcome', you extract your objectives: the 'SMARTER' goals that will define your achievements. Your primary objectives, as we discussed in **Chapter 1**, probably involve one or all of the following:

- Building the reputation of the practice profitably
- Growing the practice
- Getting more client work
- Improving your offering to clients
- Motivating people.

A question to ask yourself is: what stands in the way of us realising our big, audacious goal? Great executives set big goals, then steer the business towards the goal, closing the gaps that exist between what they want to achieve and what their organisation can deliver at a given time. We can learn from this way of thinking.

Understanding the obstacles that stand in your way helps you to bridge the gap between your end goals or objectives, and where you are now. The actions prompted by a Gaps analysis and a SWOT analysis are the means to help you achieve your big, audacious goal.

Figure 4. Aiming for your end goal

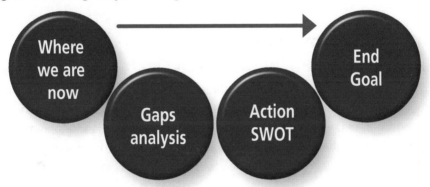

'SWOT' analysis is a practical tool to help you to identify gaps, and opportunities, for your practice. SWOT stands for 'Strengths, Weaknesses, Opportunities and Threats'. The SWOT analysis is a review of your practice to find out which **strengths** can contribute to the success of your chosen objectives, and whether there are inherent **weaknesses** that might prevent you from achieving your vision. Your practice is part of a wider environment. Carefully examine which external **threats** from competitors, the economy, or a decline in demand could prevent you from achieving your goals. Then there are the **opportunities** for your practice, which you need to be aware of in order to harness and exploit them.

Frank Maguire, co-founder of Federal Express, said that in deciding the future direction of a business, you should routinely hold three meetings:

- One to listen and learn from your clients, teams, colleagues, and people who are familiar with and have an opinion on how well or how badly your practice is performing.
- The second meeting is to ask the question: what are we doing that we should not be doing?
- The third meeting is to ask: what are we *not* doing that we *could* be doing?[5]

---

5. Direct quote from Frank Maguire, co-Founder of FedEx. From a presentation given to Dublin Chamber of Commerce members on 2 December 2009

This gaps analysis exercise is about 'business unusual', not business as usual

For the purposes of business development, I suggest that you take a slightly different approach to the SWOT analysis from that normally taken by marketing planners. The ordinary SWOT simply identifies strengths, weaknesses, opportunities and threats that apply to the business. In the current market or environment, action is most important, so I suggest that you conduct an **Action SWOT**.

How is the Action SWOT different?

The **Action SWOT** alters your mindset from the basic approach of identifying strengths and weaknesses, and external threats and opportunities, to a much more developed thought process. The Action SWOT requires you to question how you can use strengths, defeat weaknesses, harness opportunities, and plan for and mitigate the potential risks in the market. This is not a statement of SWOT; it is a plan to make the SWOT work for you. Your SWOT analysis changes from being the standard four-box grid of bullet points to an infinitely valuable matrix to help you bridge your gaps, harness the chances that come your way, and put into action the steps to achieve your big, audacious goal.

In this context, SWOT analysis becomes a more useful chart to help you identify internal and external forces that could assist you in achieving your objectives – or prevent you from achieving them. Now you can examine your business or practice to identify how you can be radically different and better than your competitors, how you can use the market to drive your business, and how you can overcome those gaps to become better and stronger as a practice.

I have amended the traditional SWOT analysis to be an action plan to help you achieve your goals. Actions provide the answers to these four issues:

- **How we use our strengths**

- **How we overcome weaknesses**

- **How we harness opportunities**

- **How we mitigate potential threats.**

Look at your practice and ask: what makes you stand out as different from others who offer the same type of service as you? What specialist skills do you provide that no one else does? What do you do for clients that they particularly approve of, comment on, or mention to others? Conversely, are there areas that need significant improvement in order for you to compete successfully in the current market? This is your opportunity to define the reality of what you offer to clients.

You want clients to see your best side. You don't necessarily have to be liked a lot, but you do have to be trusted, and a client has to consider you the right person or firm for the job in hand. There is a certain amount of charm required. In most cases, this bonhomie does not happen by accident. How do you convince a client, or potential client, that you are the best in your field, that you are the most suitable for their needs, and that you are the one who will represent their interests in the best way possible?

First of all, find out why your clients attend your practice. (You probably recorded this in the notes when you first met them.) If they have remained loyal to you, find out why. Ask them. Be prepared for some interesting answers. In fact, every person who comes through your door can teach you something about your business – whether they avail of your service or not. So take note of the response from those who choose to use your services – and, importantly, those who do not.

Next, keep a note of the problems that those people need to resolve. Be aware of why new clients choose you above other suppliers. Understand the difference between your approach and that of your competitors. Where are you considered better, where are you not? That insight will give you ideas on how to recruit other clients.

If you haven't already, call the customers who no longer do business with your firm. Again, log the reasons why your past clients chose to go to other providers or no longer deal with you. What problems could your practice not solve for them?

Figure 5. Action SWOT

2. How we use our strengths

While conducting your SWOT analysis, identify the unusual strengths in your business. Consult with your team and your clients, then succinctly and realistically commit the results to paper. The aim is to focus on areas of expertise and to isolate the unique capabilities within your practice. Consider the strengths that make you unique. Think about the value you give to clients that puts you ahead of the competition. Incorporate the skills that are, or could be, compelling in the marketplace.

Be specific. These are areas that are within your control and that give you an edge over your competitors. They might include specialist skills, local profile, client loyalty and location.

3. How we overcome weaknesses

Similarly, by highlighting any weaknesses in your organisation, you will see more clearly where you are vulnerable to your competitors. If you are not absolutely clear about your own deficiencies, others certainly will be. Weaknesses may include premises that are not up to standard, perceived low customer service standards, or internal conflict within your organisation.

Adopt a high-level vision of your practice – 'a helicopter view'. Weaknesses should be taken from the feedback provided by existing and past clients, by colleagues, and by people in your community. Only when you find out how you are really perceived can you address any inherent weaknesses.

4. How we harness opportunities

These are external factors, as discussed in the previous chapter, that are beyond your control but which could yield useful opportunities for your practice. Areas to consider include new or amended legislation, which is often a source of significant income for professional advisors. Examine changes in demographics, which include the aging population or an increasing ethnic population. Market trends, such as the growth of eco-friendly or cost-conscious consumers, are also useful opportunities.

5. How we mitigate potential threats

Threats are also external factors that are beyond your control, but which can pose difficulties or challenges for your practice. Consider any potential threats that could derail your business. Areas to consider include a significant decline in a particular market sector, such as construction, for example. Also, think about how the possibility of a short-term decline in population might affect your business because a significant proportion of young people are once again emigrating to countries that offer them better opportunities.

Test Case

Case Study 1: Accountancy Firm Action SWOT

Here is a synopsis of an Action SWOT developed for an accountancy firm:

Our firm is the largest in a big town. We have never had to do much marketing, but lately our business has tapered off, due to the recession. Because some of our clients are experiencing financial difficulties, they are no longer doing the level of business with us that they used to. Competition has also intensified, and other larger accountancy firms from other areas are beginning to come into our territory, offering discounts to local business. We know that the market will turn around, and we want to be ready to take advantage of the upturn.

Our big, audacious objective is to grow our client base by 5 percent in the coming year by implementing a 'switcher' campaign. Why? Because we believe that there are new clients out there: people who are no longer satisfied with what their existing firm offers – firms that don't offer the range of services that we do and that don't have the same satisfaction ratings that we have.

Looking at our business, here are the strengths, weaknesses, opportunities and threats that we identified.

STRENGTHS

Community players. We are in the area for twenty years. We employ a local, highly skilled team and we have established strong community relationships with clients and the business community.

Client relationships. We spend time with each individual client, getting to know their needs and looking for ways to help them do better.

Cost-effective. Outsourcing routine work to local sole practitioners allows us to operate in a very cost-effective way for clients who cannot afford to pay a lot for basic accountancy services.

WEAKNESSES

Marketing. Traditionally, we have not focused on promoting ourselves in the local community because word-of-mouth was our best marketing tool. Business just came to us, in the form of clients referred by other clients. Now we find ourselves having to develop a profile to promote our services to a wider catchment area.

Online accounting facility for clients. We want our clients to be able to link with us online in the near future but have not done so yet.

CRM. We don't have a centralised client relationship management (CRM) system in place. Each partner has his or her own set of contacts.

OPPORTUNITIES

Our relationships. We have built excellent relationships with the external community over time. We have to take the opportunity to maximise those relationships now, to get introductions to more businesses locally and in the extended area.

Market sectors. There are a number of market segments in the entrepreneurship sector that we have not targeted specifically to date, but we are already doing good work for clients of those sectors. These include local industry, retailers, and farmers who are seeking to diversify their income streams.

Collaboration. Other local businesses are eager to network in the current market, and we have the opportunity to work with business and community organisations, bankers, solicitors and other businesses to create networking opportunities. We would like to spearhead this in our community.

THREATS

Competition. The small, low-cost operators are very evident in the marketplace – sole practitioners who are undercutting us for particular services. Even the heavy hitters are competing in our space for business that was not a high priority for them in the past. As a mid-size player, we are at risk.

Lower margins. Intensified competition has put a squeeze on margins.

Online capability. Clients are increasingly availing of online packages for accounting. We need to be able to compete in this area or there is a risk that we will be left behind.

Action SWOT

To achieve our 5 percent practice growth objective for 2011, we need to take the following action to target the entrepreneur segment of the market.

Figure 6. Action SWOT (Developed from Case Study)

How we use our strengths	How we overcome weaknesses
• Research what makes our client relationships excellent and build on that • Become the recognised thought-leaders in the community by taking key speaker opportunities at conferences • Seek out ways to be more cost-effective	• Put a programme of local marketing in place • Implement an online accounting facility • Immediately identify a suitable CRM package for the firm
How we harness opportunities	**How we mitigate potential threats**
• Build on networking opportunities in a formal way • Look at how we can further outsource low-value processes • Work to develop an in-depth understanding of the new local industry that is developing in our wider catchment area – particularly tapping into the farming sector	• Understand and monitor competitor activity carefully • Collaborate with the key influencers in the town and surrounding areas to cement our community presence further • Find ways to add value and communicate the value of products and services we offer • Develop our online capability for entrepreneurs so that it is the best that is available in the market

The purpose of the above case study is to demonstrate the types of marketing activity you can pursue to improve your business, and how quickly you can do this. This is just a brief synopsis for illustration purposes. The various types of marketing activity that you can engage in will be discussed in far greater detail in later chapters.

The main message for this chapter is that this is a time for action, not strategic analysis/paralysis. Set your objectives, identify the gaps that prevent you from getting there, and treat your SWOT as a prompt for activity that will help you to build the bridge between your current position and your desired outcome.

Applied Science

Project Plan

Having set your objective, put in place a project plan to address the gaps that you have identified. List five main outcomes that you want to achieve. Each **outcome** is the result of bridging a gap that you have identified. Schedule the **activity** that you or your team need to engage in to deliver your desired outcome. Then clearly delineate the **tasks** that are required to help you reach that outcome. It is vital to set benchmarks and **measure** your progress. (See the sample Project Plan on page 31.)

Figure 7: Here are five sample actions for your Project Plan.

Outcome	Activity	Actions	Tasks	Measure	By when	Done ✓
1. Build reputation	Client servicing	Ensure every client satisfied with service	1. Make it clear to clients what services *are* provided 2. Make it clear to clients what services *are not* provided 3. Deliver exceptional service	Conduct an annual survey to measure how satisfied clients are	[Date]	
2. Profit	Service offering	Deliver services that provide a return on input	1. Identify services that are highly profitable 2. Identify services that are not profitable 3. Find ways to deliver unprofitable services at a profit by automation or outsourcing	Evaluate the profitability of product and service delivery	[Date]	
3. Grow the practice	Sales	Increase the number of paying and profitable clients	1. Go to chamber networking evening 3 June 2. Hold a seminar for 12 prospective clients 2 May 3. Host or sponsor a local community event	Measure number and value of new paying clients	[Date]	
4. Increase client work	Cross selling	Increase the billable hours per client	1. Manage client relationship, and identify and satisfy their needs profitably	Measure number of products or services per client	[Date]	
5. Team motivation	Employee engagement	Build employee motivation	1. Use performance recognition to reward employees	Measured by employee retention, sick leave, commitment and advocacy	[Date]	

Review dates

Set defined review dates for completion of the various aspects of your project plan. When you go through a planning process like this one outlined in **Figure 7**, there may be aspects of your firm or practice that inhibit the outcome and which present gaps that need to be bridged. One accountancy firm that I met found that clients could not get hold of their relationship managers by phone, and that was considered to be poor service. The firm decided to advise their clients that they would always be available for phone calls for a defined period, e.g. between 2pm and 4pm each day. The feedback from clients regarding service improved significantly. **Figure 8** suggests the format of a useful milestone chart for recording your progress.

Figure 8. A milestone plan

Milestones Six-month Plan	Jan	Feb	Mar	Apr	May	Jun
Gap 1 – Clients cannot access relationship managers by phone	■	■				
Gap 2 – Some services are unprofitable			■			
Gap 3 – Need to increase volume of profitable clients	■	■	■	■		
Gap 4 – Product penetration per client is low					■	
Gap 5 – Employees are not advocates of the practice						■

Customer Relationship Management: 3
Five ways to find new clients

'The aim of marketing is to know and understand the customer so well that the product or service fits him and sells itself.'

Peter Drucker

Marketing helps you to connect with people and to stand out, to be different from your competitors. Marketing is about your profile in the community, your understanding of the market in which you operate, your communications, and your customer relationship management (or 'CRM'). CRM is about how you manage your relationship with existing clients, and how to develop and track leads for prospective clients.

I asked every professional that I interviewed for **Client Science** what they do to get client work. As you might expect, business development came up as the greatest challenge for every professional that I met, and without exception. It is for this reason that I have chosen to present here, near the start of the book, some ideas to help you to stimulate business. I recognise that most professionals are eager, if not anxious, to generate more business from existing and new clients.

Data Protection

Some of what I discuss in this chapter relates to how you hold on to client records, how you follow up with existing clients for more business and how you network to acquire new clients. At this point it is important to mention the Data Protection Acts which particularly impact businesses and professional practitioners who are targeting individuals as clients – these are often referred to as 'personal customers'. The Data Protection Act was brought into force in Ireland in 1988 with an amendment in 2003. It was also introduced in the UK in 1998.

When you are communicating with personal clients, and these include individuals and sole traders operating in business, then you must observe the rules of Data Protection. Here are five critical things you should know about data protection:

- Obtain and process information fairly. Ensure that individuals are aware of why you have their personal data and how it will be used. Give them a copy of that information upon request.

- When you ask an individual for personal data, only use that information for the purposes that you specified when you asked them for it. Do not use that information for other marketing or cross-selling purposes without their express permission.

- Do not pass the information you receive to a third party without the agreement of the individual.

- Retain the information only for as long as is necessary and no longer.

- Refer to the Data Protection Legislation that relates to your jurisdiction: Ireland www.dataprotection.ie; UK www.ico.gov.uk

Using CRM to build your business

Most of the people I interviewed either told me about or showed me their CRM system. CRM systems keep your client and prospective client records in one accessible place. Some people showed me notebooks, others had spreadsheets, and some professionals had CRM packages specifically designed for their firm. Most people agreed that they performed better with some form of computerised system in place.

So what are the five ways in which you can use CRM wisely to get more client work?

- The first is to set up a suitable Customer Relationship Management or CRM system that allows you to track your interactions with existing clients, and to compile useful data about your potential clients.

- Secondly, put a sales pipeline in place. A sales pipeline is simply a report or a spreadsheet that tracks the names that you are targeting for new business.

- Thirdly, gain a full understanding of the market in which you operate: the politics, legislation, technology, socio-economic and environmental factors that present challenges and opportunities.

- Then network, so that you can get to know a cross-section of your prospective clients. There are networking tips for you in this chapter so that you can find new people to target.

- The fifth way to use CRM effectively is to look out for market trends that could help you to target segments that are actually growing rather than stagnating or in decline.

Figure 9. Customer Relationship Management: Five ways to get more work

1. Install a CRM system

2. Establish a sales pipeline

3. Understand your market

4. Network to generate new leads

5. Watch out for market trends

1. Install a CRM system

If you do not already have one, a good quality CRM system should be the lead item on your agenda for this year. Find a simple and systematic way of collecting client data from all points of contact and storing them in one data pool. When implementing a CRM system, make sure that you observe the Data Protection Act which affects your ability to market to individual clients and sole traders (see above).

Usually, information relating to interactions with a client is stored in your order-processing or invoicing systems, your sales- and contact-management systems (such as appointment calendars), databases for customer communications (such as Christmas card lists), newsletter databases or lists of names invited to various client events. Good quality CRM systems are designed to bring all of this information together into one **shared** system that records interactions with clients, invitations to events, communications, services provided and amounts invoiced to each particular client.[6]

---

6.   Nigel Piercey. *Market-led Strategic Change.* (Butterworth-Heinemann, 2000)

While most of the professionals that I interviewed know who their best clients are, few had a clear picture of all of their clients at an individual level. A good quality CRM system will enable you to keep records of past clients and their transactions, and current clients and all interactions and communications with them. You can also record potential client opportunities.

I recommend that you research and find a good CRM system that has the capability to expand as your practice grows. There are several excellent CRM systems available which are simple to use, relatively inexpensive and, in many cases, accessible online, so that they can be easily installed. (For example, SalesForce.com is one of the most popular online systems, and it is used worldwide.)

The benefits of installing even the most basic customer database are immense. It is a way of pulling together all the information that you already have on your existing and past clients so that you can reference it quickly and efficiently. This is a great way of retaining the details of past clients, long after their file is closed, subject to rules of the Data Protection Acts. It allows you to contact them again, without having to trudge through your archives for their details. The Data Protection legislation only allows you to retain records for individuals and sole traders who are existing clients. You should not use their details to market new products or services to them, without having sought their permission in writing and in advance. Where business or non-sole trader clients are concerned, your CRM system is useful for keeping records of client businesses whose details might otherwise be forgotten and lost forever.

A database can integrate your past, present and prospective clients to give you a full picture of your target market. I find this the most useful feature of a CRM system. It means that the full spectrum of clients that you could tap into for business is always in front of you. This includes your existing clients, those you did business with in the past, and those you have on your target list for the future.

A good database gives you the facility to update the files with new information on individual clients and prospective clients as it becomes available. Most importantly, as you network, it allows you to be constantly aware of who you are targeting and to be on the lookout for opportunities to introduce yourself to the names you have on your prospect list.

CRM systems enable you to hold details about existing clients such as email addresses, telephone numbers and contact addresses, all in one place. Again, remember to observe the Data Protection legislation and get approval from clients and potential clients before you record their personal details on your database for marketing and communication purposes. At the click of a mouse, you can send newsletters, communication updates, or invitations by email. Or you can print off address labels for more formal correspondence, if that better suits your purposes.

A good CRM system enables you to record all interactions with potential clients. This allows you or your team to find out whether a person has been approached by your practice or not, and whether they might be receptive to a call. It allows you to schedule future appointment dates, and it can set up a reminder on your calendar to let you know when that contact date arrives.

CRM will provide you with the latest update of your sales pipeline, which can be defined as a list of the potential clients that you are targeting. It is vital that you have a pipeline of potential clients, people that you intend to contact or have contacted, and meetings that you have set up. An effective CRM system should have the facility to store this information, and it should allow you to produce regular reports.

2. Establish a sales pipeline

It is very important when you are embarking on a business development programme to establish a sales pipeline. A sales pipeline is simply a report or spreadsheet that tracks the names that you are targeting for new business.

The table or spreadsheet in **Figure 10** below is an example of a sales pipeline. You can code the names that you are targeting as red, amber or green. Your **red** names are at the early stage of the sales cycle: names that you would like to recruit as clients, and names that you plan to make an appointment to meet. **Amber** names are people that you have made contact with. They have indicated interest in your service, and you have sent them details and pricing. **Green** names have indicated that they will do business with you.

Applied Science

Complete this table as fully as you possibly can. Insert details about your **contact** person, their **title** and the **company** they belong to. State the **opportunity type**, which is whether the potential client is a new or existing prospect. Estimate the amount of **revenue** that you can earn from the client; this can generally only be entered when you have had discussions with the prospective client about their requirements.

Enter a **weighting** for each client. You may estimate that an **amber** client is 80 percent likely to do some business with you, or that a **red** client is 30 percent likely to do business with you. As the contact moves from **red** to **amber** to **green,** their weighting increases.

Figure 10. A sales pipeline

Sales Person	Contact	Title	Company	Date Entered	Opport-unity Type	Revenue	Product/ Service	Descrip-tion	Weight-ing	Green Amber Red	Forecast Date	Comment
					New/ Existing					Green		
										Amber		
										Red		

Source: Fiona Flynn, Sales Solutions

A good rule of thumb is to ensure a minimum of three purposeful marketing contacts per week and maintain a network of approximately forty referral sources to keep your practice healthy.[7] Your pipeline should contain a minimum of twenty-five new contacts at all times.

3. Understand your market

We all have a far more sophisticated awareness of the marketplace than we realise. Information about it comes at us at an incredible rate from news, advertising, conversation, correspondence, TV, radio and the Internet. The problem you face is not how much you know about your market, your clients and your target clients but how to distil that information so that it will help you to achieve your goals and attract the sort of client work that you are looking for.

One challenge is not to get bogged down in market intelligence. There is a lot of data available; some of it is highly relevant, some is nice to know, but most is not useful to you at all. Too much information can lead to inertia. I recommend a two-page

---

7. Mark Powers and Shawn McNalis, *How Good Attorneys become Great Rainmakers* (Independently published 2009)

document that contains the key market analysis metrics as they specifically relate to your objectives. The market metrics that relate to most professionals are outlined below and they include political and legal developments, economic data, demographic and sociological information and technological updates. This critical information should be easily updatable as new information becomes available. If there is detailed information that you need to refer to in more depth, attach that as an Appendix to your plan.

Applied Science

'The best market information that I have received through the years takes the form of snippets of news, subjective views, throwaway remarks, client comments and informal information gathered by members of the team and those closest to the actual market. Don't rely totally on formal research or statistics to lead you to the Holy Grail.

Also, the best way to do business in a local community is to do business with the local people. If you are a customer of the butcher, the baker, the local shop, then you have a much better chance of them becoming a client.'

Business banker

The annual Budget announcements by the Minister for Finance tell you whether there have been amendments to stamp duty rates for first-time buyers, for example. The Retail Sales Index tells you whether consumers are spending more or less. Inflation rates tell you whether prices are going up or coming down. When you read the market, your aim is to keep up to date with relevant developments that directly or indirectly affect your practice, and easily pull together a snapshot of the market you operate in.

What do I mean by 'operate in'? Either you control your market environment or it controls you. If you stay well-informed and measured in your approach, and you are adaptable to market changes as they arise, then you can operate in the market. If you don't stay informed, you are at risk from competitors who are more adaptable than you.

It is important that you are keenly aware of upcoming changes in the market as early as possible so that you can adapt your operation to meet the changing needs of your clients. You have to be ahead of the game wherever possible, because it is your understanding of the market that will lead you to your best opportunities to offer new services, to new clients, in a new and interesting way. This is what competitive advantage is all about.

Science
Fact 'Legislative and regulatory changes are extremely lucrative for professionals. Take Sarbanes–Oxley, for example: an entire industry grew up around the implementation of those revised accounting practices, and the people who learned how to implement them first made a fortune showing everyone else.'

Accountant

Under each of the headings – political, economic, social, technological, legislative and environmental – always be aware of new developments that affect your practice. Here are some examples:

Political

Thousands of opportunities for professionals come from the political system every year. The increased focus on our 'Carbon Footprint', changes in taxation, and even the flu vaccine from the health service represent opportunities for professionals. Be aware of political trends, changes and directives at a national and local level and from the European Union.

Economic

There is no shortage of economic data. The critical thing is to carefully choose the metrics that guide the development of your business and to keep a record of those metrics. Economic data can be drawn from Central Bank reports, the Central Statistics Office (CSO), ESRI reports, ECB updates, and financial papers and websites such as Reuters or Bloomberg. Link in with an economist, perhaps one connected to your bank or stockbroking firm, and request that they send you their regular economic bulletins. All of these sources provide economic updates and forecasts, trends and market analysis. While it is almost impossible to be absolutely accurate in forecasting the market, having relevant economic data to hand can help to inform your thinking.

Social

The social aspect of your market review refers to an analysis of social relations, social stratification, social interaction and culture. They are important if they in some way have an impact on your professional services. Over the last number of years, the growth in Ireland's multi-ethnic population has presented new opportunities for professionals. The ageing population is an important and growing market trend worldwide. The dynamic youth market may also present challenges and opportunities for you.

Technological

Read up on or get advice on technological advances that could affect your practice. Systems, communications, and website functionality jump forward in leaps and bounds every few months. The pace of change in technology is phenomenal. Many of your clients, particularly those under the age of thirty-five, have a high expectation that service suppliers will have a high quality website, will provide services where possible, and communicate using the latest technology. According to Nigel Piercey, author and professor at the Cranford Business School:

'In an era where the Internet is daily fuelling the blurring of traditional product–market boundaries, there is nothing fixed or static about the definition of the market where you hope to earn a living.' [8]

If you are not particularly knowledgeable about the latest technology, I suggest that you get to know people who are up-to-date and who can keep you well-informed on the latest developments. There are thousands of people who are experts in this area; they can help you with CRM systems, online presence, and the automation of routine services, where appropriate.

Legislative

Changes in legislation, regulations or EU Directives can present tremendous opportunities for all professionals, but especially legal and accountancy experts. Legislative changes can also present costly challenges for professionals such as those involved in the banking and construction sectors. It makes sense to understand the implications of legislation relating to your area and, very importantly, those relating to your clients and potential clients.

Environmental

The environment is big news at the moment, and it is likely to remain an area with opportunities for professional practitioners. There are certainly opportunities for business development for almost all professionals in practice. It is well worth developing expertise where possible in your area relating to bio-energy, the bio-medical field, waste management, and the protection of the environment.

---

8.   Nigel Piercey, *Market-led Strategic Change* (as above)

There may also be aspects of the environment that will have an adverse effect on your business. For example, flooding has become a huge area of concern in recent years.

4. Network to generate new leads

One of the greatest benefits of a CRM system is storing the names of potential leads. But how do you get those names? I'm not a fan of cold-calling. In my experience, networking produces far better, 'warmer' leads. (By 'networking', I mean generating target contact names of people who have confirmed to you that they are positively receptive to a call from you.)

One of the most obvious signs of the economic downturn is the surge in numbers signing up for networking events. In these leaner times, networking by professionals has taken on a far greater significance. The struggle for new clients to replace a declining client base now poses a far graver challenge for professionals than rising costs or even access to finance due to the 'credit crunch'.

So, how do you access the names that you want to target? The answer is to **build alliances**. To attract more profitable clients; you need to identify the characteristics of a profitable client; then determine who influences this type of client, and thirdly, market yourself to these influencers. These influencers may be their professional body, their local Chambers of Commerce, Rotary Club, Enterprise Board or training college.

Forge relationships with the organisations in your community that have the greatest influence over your particular target market. If your target audience is parents with children, get involved with the local schools. If your target audience is companies that are exporting and importing, build an alliance with the organisations that help business and service providers to trade abroad, such as the Irish Exporters' Association. If your target audience is the farming sector, then join forces with Macra na Feirme.

Find out what you have to do to get in front of your target clients. How do they communicate? Is it primarily through online social networking, or do they hold conferences and seminars? Do your prospective clients subscribe to particular journals, periodicals or magazines? Where do they hang out? What will draw them to you?

There is networking and there is '**real networking**'. Real networking is getting to the decision-maker, and it is far more targeted than the sort of networking that places you in a big conference hall hoping that you'll just bump into the right people. Real networking takes some thought and planning.

Be clear about who you want to target. Know your target audience well and have your research done so that you always have a target in mind. That might be getting to one important decision-maker or ten – but it should not be random.

In his book, *Rain Making*, Ford Harding says that there is more time wasted on what is claimed to be networking than on any other area of professional services. He describes this as a disturbing scenario because it is not just the out-of-pocket expenses that are wasted, but also the total cost of those lost billable hours plus the opportunity cost of not using networking properly.[9]

One of the fundamental rules of networking is that it involves **helping people**. In varying circumstances, leads, information on prospects, introductions, sales assistance, references and ideas are some of the kinds of help provided by networkers.[10] The greatest networkers are extremely helpful. They always know someone who knows someone who can solve a problem. They ask 'what can I do for you?' not 'what can you do for me?' They build trust in this way. They are patient, not desperate. They exude confidence and capability.

You have to build your network in that way. Be a force for good in an ever-widening circle. Get to know people. Use your talents for the good of others. Then, as you identify the decision-makers that you need in order to realise your own goals, call on the people in your circle to open those doors for you. Now you are into the arena of warm leads, not cold calls.

Be conscious too that you can create networking opportunities for your clients or potential clients. There are literally hundreds of organisations whose members would be delighted to attend a seminar where their local professional is speaking on a topic relevant to their needs, or concerns, or that helps them to shed further light on a particular topic that interests them. In the eyes of many people, you have the benefit of being an expert, and people can very often gain from your wisdom and your understanding of your specialist area. This is very valuable.

When you join forces with other organisations, and even when you attend networking evenings or social evenings scheduled by community groups, you will very often meet people that you can add to your target client list. These are the 'warm leads' that are so valuable because people that you exchange a business card with are familiar with your name and your profile. These are the people that are more likely to answer your call for business in the future.

---

9. Ford Harding, *Rain Making* (Adams Business, 2008)
10. Ford Harding, *Rain Making* (as above)

There is more in-depth information on personal selling and networking in **Chapter 12**.

5. Watch out for Market trends

Keeping up to date with the latest market influences and cultural trends could have a major impact on your practice. The first thing to consider is what are the upcoming trends you should be aware of when you are looking for more business from your existing clients, or targeting prospective ones. The second important consideration is that, as their trusted advisor, your clients expect you to be up to date on market developments and to have the sort of understanding that allows them to rely on you to keep them informed.

Here are five trends for the next decade:

- Eco-friendly products and services and initiatives oriented towards protecting the environment

- Frugality due to reduced income levels, lessons learned in the boom, and a decrease in the value of assets

- Ageing population as the baby boomers move into old age

- Market gardening and a back-to-basics approach to living

- Healthcare and alternative medicine continue to be a growth sector.

Science Fiction

You can't be prepared for every scenario, as this story illustrates

The annual crowning of a goat as king of Ireland at one of the country's oldest fairs was in doubt in 2009 after organisers said that the heir to the throne might be stopped from travelling to the festival due to a visa problem.

Traditionally, a male goat is caught in the mountains of Kerry and paraded through the town of Killorglin, where he reigns for the three days of the Puck Fair, a centuries-old festival of drinking, music and dancing.

The problem was that the chosen animal for that year was from the Northern Ireland town of Ballycastle. The Puck Fair organising committee could only get a four-day licence for the trip south of the border, and they needed the goat for five days.

'It takes at least a day to bring a goat from Ballycastle to Killorglin and a day to bring it back. Then the goat is on the stand for three days. It's not possible to do all that within a four-day visa,' said Puck Fair chairman Declan Mangan. 'The people in Ballycastle are looking for another goat with an extended visa to come to Kerry next year.'[11]

11. Padraic Halpin, Reuters, 24 July 2009

Clients:
Five important client insights

4

*'The client has the power to fire you
by simply walking away.'*

Sam Walton, founder of Wal-Mart

Over the past two decades, there has been a 'power shift' towards consumers. More aggressive competition, consumer protection legislation and greater educational and travel opportunities have helped business and personal customers develop a greater understanding of their buying power in the market. This current generation of clients recognises how valuable they are and how important they are to a professional practice. Millions of Euro have been spent on advertisements luring people to switch banks, insurance companies and even solicitors in recent years – which shows how much power and choice customers now have. Consumers are enticed by advertising telling them that they can find a better deal if they are prepared to look around. People in business are wooed by phone calls and visits from professionals hoping to attract new clients.

In the modern market, clients who choose to take their business elsewhere can do so in a matter of minutes, and all that's involved in some cases is the click of a mouse.

This increased consumer confidence has implications for all professionals in practice. The fact that clients are more willing to switch suppliers means that it can be much harder to engender loyalty among clients and to know for certain which clients are likely to remain loyal. In the past, you might have been guaranteed the lifetime loyalty of a high proportion of your clients, but you cannot assume that today.

Top Scientist

While the previous chapters focused on what you, as a leader of your firm, want to achieve for your practice, the objective of this chapter is to help you to gain a greater insight into the value of your clients.

Science Fact

In his book, *The Loyalty Effect*, Frederick F. Reichheld argues that loyalty is the most important factor in the success of a business. He cites loyalty of clients, loyalty of employees and loyalty of investors as being critical. His research shows that the average company loses between 10 and 30 percent of its clients every year. He also calculates that a 5 percent

Client Science – The Five Cs Marketing Plan for Professionals

improvement in client-retention rates could yield an increase in profits of between 25 and 100 percent.[12]

The crucial question is: do you have a complete picture of the value of each individual client to your practice? Clients tell you a lot about your practice: they feed back to you verbally, they inform you by their actions, and they send you subconscious messages about whether they value your service or not. 'Reading' client feedback is critical to the success of your practice. You can use your insight into clients to help you to improve your service, your processes and your communication.

Here are the five insights that this chapter will help you get from your clients:

Figure 11. Clients: Five important client insights

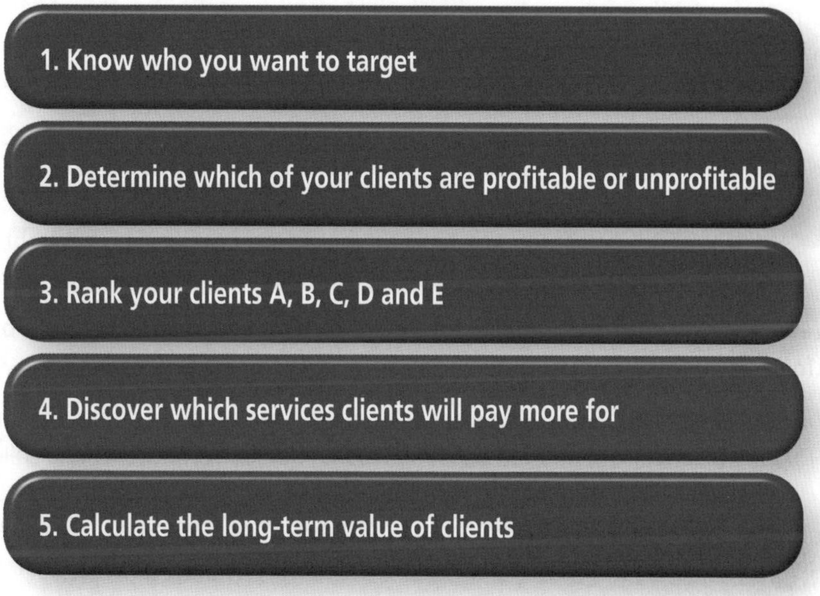

> **1. Know who you want to target**

> **2. Determine which of your clients are profitable or unprofitable**

> **3. Rank your clients A, B, C, D and E**

> **4. Discover which services clients will pay more for**

> **5. Calculate the long-term value of clients**

1. Know who you want to target

When you establish a practice in a particular location, at first you are much more likely to evaluate your neighbourhood, to take account of who your potential client base could be. In other words, you have a tremendous interest in finding out who the audience is for your message about your practice. This tends to change, once you are established. The professionals that I spoke to were less inclined to review the range

---

12. Frederick F. Reichheld, *The Loyalty Effect* (Harvard Business School Press, 1996)

of prospective clients in their marketplace all over again. However, the new economic climate led a number of firms to become once again more outward-focused, and many had begun the (re-)evaluation process in earnest.

There are several ways to take stock of the potential clients in your area. If your client base tends to be made up of individuals or personal clients, get a map and review local housing estates and apartment blocks. Be aware of the size, location and characteristics of the neighbourhood communities that you are targeting. Take account of the local newspapers that residents receive. Note their local Chambers and community activity groups. All will be useful to you when you are promoting your services at a later date.

If your target audience is business clients, map your territory. Identify the areas that have the best potential for your business: towns, industrial estates or farming areas, for example. Circle the locations that are top of your priority list. Then, most importantly, obtain as much detailed information on those particular businesses as possible, so that you understand who influences them, the type of services that they require, and how you can most appropriately approach them.

Be very much aware of the requirements of the Data Protection legislation. Instead of approaching people whom you do not know, and who are not acquainted with you, get an introduction to your target name. This is called a 'warm lead'. The success rates of approaching clients to whom you have obtained an introduction are infinitely higher than cold-calling.

Science Fact

To create long-term sustainability for your practice, you need a broadly-based portfolio of clients.

The best way to develop a wide range of clients is to target sectors of the market that lead to good balance. I mentioned above that some banks, accountants and solicitors experienced great difficulty with the collapse of the property sector because they were over-reliant on it for their business. One lesson here is to diversify. You need to service a carefully selected number of sectors so that if one or two go into decline, the others continue to supply business.

Applied Science

'Our firm developed relationships overseas consistently during the past ten years. We built up contacts with law firms in the UK and in the United States. Firms abroad who have legal business relating to Ireland refer their clients to us. We have a reciprocal arrangement with those firms. We are glad we maintained those relationships, because now 50 percent of our business comes from overseas, and we have not been hit by the recession here, to the same degree as other law firms.'

Lawyer

Working for new clients and new sectors helps you to build greater expertise and expand your areas of specialisation. It also helps you to preserve your business prospects in a downturn.

Understand the dynamics of the sectors that you are targeting. Get the industry journals, subscribe to publications and white papers, and attend conferences and seminars organised by the relevant associations. Over time, you will get to know the issues that prospective clients in these sectors experience, and be able to attend meetings with potential clients with real information about their issues.[13]

Applied Science

'We realised that we had a lot to offer the farming community in terms of family law, state probate, and EU legislation. We approached Macra na Feirme and developed a number of joint initiatives with that organisation, specifically to keep farmers informed of their legal rights and obligations.

One of the initiatives was a legal seminar for farmers, and two of our lawyers talked about areas of specific relevance to the audience. The question-and-answer session lasted an hour and a half. There was tremendous interest in our expertise. We received a number of legal instructions from people who attended the seminar. Seminars work particularly well for us, because people can access lawyers directly, ask questions, and discuss points of legal interest after the event. It's a great way to meet potential and existing clients.'

Lawyer

2. Profitable and unprofitable clients

Science Theory

Which of your clients are profitable and which are not profitable? You probably know how much annual income you earn from each of your clients. The problem is that income earned per client does not tell the full story.

Top Scientist

Harvard Professor Dr Robert Kaplan and Steve Anderson of Acorn Systems, based in the US, state that overall income figures can hide the true cost and profitability levels of doing business with clients. Income does not tell you how much time you spend with a client, how many introductions you get from them for new business, or how responsive they are to providing you with the essential information required to do a job. Income does not tell you how demanding a client is on your resources; it does not tell you how much it costs to service that client.

13. David Maister, *Managing Professional Services* (Free Press Business, 2003)

Research by Dr Robert Kaplan, who specialises in profitability analysis, explains this concept further. The Pareto principle, also known as the '**20:80 Rule**', holds true for many business phenomena: 20 percent of the products account for 80 percent of sales; the top 20 percent of customers generate 80 percent of revenues. But the Pareto 20:80 rule does not apply to profits as illustrated by **the 'Whale Curve'** (see **Figure 12**). The most profitable 20 percent of products and customers generally produce between 150 and 300 percent of profits.

Figure 12. The 'Whale Curve'

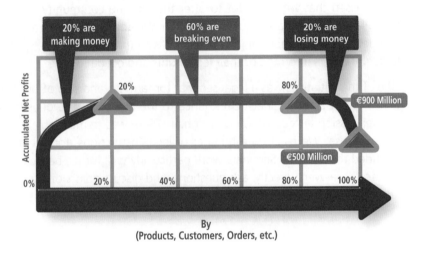

Image courtesy of Dr Robert Kaplan and Acorn Systems Inc., USA

Science Theory The high profitability of the top tier of customers balances out the unprofitable lower tier of customers, to reach the final 100 percent profitability figure. The Whale Curve graphically illustrates how:

- The most profitable 20 percent of clients could deliver between 150 and 300 percent of profits. In other words, if the business attracted only the most profitable clients, profits could be increased up to threefold.

- The middle 60 percent of clients are at break-even level.

- The least profitable 20 percent of clients lose your practice between 50 and 200 percent of total profits and, therefore, they wipe out the benefit of the profits made from the most profitable 20 percent of clients.

Test Case
This means that some of your largest clients could turn out to be the most unprofitable.[14]

How do Robert Kaplan's findings apply to your practice? If you examine the cost of all the resources devoted to individual clients, you will discover that some clients cost you much more to serve than others, even though they all may deliver approximately the same revenues. This means that when you evaluate your clients and see that you earn more income from some than from others, you have to look also at the level of input that was required by your firm and how much that input cost. The value of a particular client can alter considerably when you factor in how much it costs to serve that client.

Case study 2: ABC Building Society

In the 1990s, one Irish building society recognised that they had a significant problem in their branches with their cost-to-serve ratio. Their branch-based employees spent a large proportion of their time dealing with long queues of people waiting to conduct routine transactions such as cash lodgements, cheque cashing and bill payments. Executives identified that high transaction-based account activity did not necessarily correlate with high deposit value. In fact, those customers with high deposits visited the branches less.

This focus on transactional services affected the society's ability to deal with customers who needed mortgage and investment advice. These were in fact the most important and most profitable aspects of the building society's business. The main issue was that employees were not spending enough time servicing profitable customers because they were forced to deal with queues of people waiting to make routine transactions.

So, the executive team decided to take the brave and somewhat unusual step of becoming a 'bank with no cash'.

This strategic decision could not work without a programme in place to support the customers who depended on them for cash transactions. Thus, over a period of time, they provided their customers with the best alternatives possible to handle their routine transactions. In many cases, the alternatives were far better for the customer than having to stand in a queue at a branch for hours.

---

14. Dr Robert Kaplan, "Measuring and Managing Customer Profitability", *Journal of Cost Management* (Sep/Oct 2001): 5-15. V.G. Narayanan.

The alternatives included:

- Installing ATM machines at branch locations for cash withdrawal

- Telephone banking services to provide balance information, funds transfers and bill payments

- Online banking for balances, funds transfer and bill payments

- Standing order and direct debit facilities for regular incoming and outgoing payments

Over time, the bank withdrew cash-handling facilities and the queues diminished. Over the same period of time, profitability grew significantly. Staff could now focus their attention on customers and potential customers who needed mortgages and investment advice.

Having worked out which clients cost you money and which earn you money, the next step is to rank your clients, according to their true cost-to-serve value.

3. Rank your clients A, B, C, D or E

Ranking your clients need not be an overly complicated exercise; it should take the form of a high-level overview of where your clients are placed. However, it does draw your attention to which clients are outstanding and which relationships could be improved.

When evaluating the level of profitability and the cost to serve a client, here are the top five criteria that you should use:

- Fee income

- Timeliness of payment, if at all

- High or low maintenance

- Number of introductions or referrals received from the client for new business

- Overall loyalty and satisfaction with your services.

Science Experiment To rank your clients, order them from the most profitable, at the top of the list, to the least profitable, at the bottom. Almost without exception, the top 20 percent of clients are your 'A' clients, and they are usually your best advocates. Your 'A' clients require minimal administration time, they pay on time, they refer new business and they are not excessively demanding. The 'A' clients are economically significant: losing them would affect the success of your practice. Also, it would be wise to study the demographics of these individuals and target their peers as potential new clients.

B and C clients are those that receive the time and attention that they pay for. They are not highly profitable; nor are they unprofitable. They are your 'bread and butter', break-even clients. They probably represent about 70 percent of your client-base. 'B' clients have the capability of becoming 'A' clients in the future. 'C' clients often remain steady or may progress upwards with time.

At the bottom end of the spectrum are your unprofitable 'D' and 'E' ranked clients. This 10 percent of your clients are excessively demanding, require far more attention and time than they are willing to pay for and are not inclined to refer new clients to you. These clients often absorb so much of your time and resources that they become highly unprofitable to deal with. They actually cost your practice money. 'D' ranked clients consume vast swaths of your practice time and are demanding in the extreme. They do have, however, with proper management, the capability to move to become 'C' clients. 'E' clients are the ones you are better off without, in terms of revenue generation, resources and morale. They too are excessively demanding but they may not pay you at all. As such, they are non-clients.

There is a tendency among practitioners to over-service demanding clients, which is understandable. The reality is that this can cost you a significant portion of your profit.

Applied Science

So evaluate your clients, rank them as 'A', 'B', 'C', 'D' or 'E', and aim to move those that are in the 'C' and 'D' category into at least the 'B' if not the 'A' category. Carefully manage the 'E' clients out of the practice altogether.

> 'We go beyond the fees to determine who our top clients actually are. We rate clients by the length of time they have been clients of ours, the new clients they refer to us, the amount of time and resources we put into working with them and our overall relationship with them.'
>
> **Lawyer**

By eliminating your unprofitable clients, you can free up valuable hours for your team, which can be used for practice development. Consider referring out, or managing out, all of the 'D' and 'E' clients that are unlikely to become 'A', 'B' or 'C' clients. Keep in mind the long-term relationship perspective while you're doing this. At the same time, you need to be tough.

Five ways to manage 'E' clients out of your practice

It may seem contrary to everything you have ever learned, yet managing unsuitable clients out of your business may prove very important. Here are five positive approaches you could consider:

- **Do not try to 'bill these clients out the door'.** By that I mean charging them so much that they have to go elsewhere. Instead, explain that you cannot continue to serve them for the fees that they have been paying. Clearly and transparently show what you believe the account to be worth in terms of fees, and be prepared to walk away from the business if the client refuses to transact at that level.

- **Attempt to turn the situation into a win-win.** Talk it out openly with the client. Discuss the need to find a positive resolution and suggest that you will either assist them in every way you can to find alternative suppliers or that you will undertake to work with them to redress the balance.

- **Research another supplier** that better fits the requirements of your client, provide an introduction, and advise your client that the other supplier is more appropriately geared to meet their needs.

- **Do not work with unethical clients.** Occasionally, a high-paying client operates contrary to the ethics of your practice, perhaps in the form of abusing your staff, inappropriate dealings or uncooperative behaviour. It is important to discuss the issues with the client to preserve the reputation of your business. Refuse to service the client further if you feel it is necessary.

- **Avoid rush jobs, if you can.** Clients often force you to do rush jobs for them. If a client regularly insists on work being done at the last minute, it is appropriate to explain that your practice will not be in a position to take on another similar project. This gives the client time to consider how they will handle their next last-minute project.

Science Fiction

The Annual PITA Client

Each year, shortly before Christmas an accountant asks his staff to vote for the biggest PITA (pain in the ass) client – the one they would most like to lose.

The 'winning' client gets 'fired' – it's a democracy – and most years there is somebody who has upset enough staff to win by a clear margin. One of the team then drafts a tasteful letter explaining to the (now ex-) client that his business is not worth the trouble it causes.

This is one way of ensuring that the Ron Baker principle of 'Bad clients drive out the good' does not take hold too strongly.

And the effect on staff morale is immense.[15]

4. Discover which of your services clients will pay more for

Not all of your clients are the same. They have different needs and aspirations. Some want a less expensive service, less interaction with you, and their routine transactions done well. Others need specialist advice and a wider range of services. That clients have different wallets was recognised by General Motors' Alfred P. Sloan as early as 1924, when he offered the public 'a car for every purse and purpose'. GM was a pioneer of segmentation by income.[16]

Companies have been adapting their products and services to meet specifically targeted customer needs for decades. This simply means understanding that not all clients are created equal and that you have to adapt your service to suit the ones that represent the best potential for profit.

Most professionals perform a number of different services or work types for clients. Some of the work is routine and tends to be less profitable, low-margin work. Other work types require more specialist skills; they are high-margin, premium services. Clients pay more for work that is perceived as specialist or high value service, and less for more routine transactions.

If you charge for work that you do by the hour – the 'billable-hours method' – then you might find that clients strongly resist paying for routine transactions. The problem with some routine operations, such as bookkeeping, administration, writing

Applied Science

prescriptions or preparing architectural drawings, for example, is that they take a significant amount of time to do. In other words, they can be labour-intensive but clients perceive them as being of low value.

'Bookkeeping was taking up too much of our practice time, when we could be taking on more specialist high-margin accountancy work. So we outsourced all of our bookkeeping work to sole practitioners who are geared to handle that kind of work efficiently and cost-effectively.'

Accountant

---

15. Source: Barry Wilkinson on the davidmaister.com/blog/513/Firing-unprofitable-clients
16. Edward Russell-Walling, *50 Management Ideas You Really Need to Know* (Quercus Publishing, 2007)

The best course of action is to identify which aspects of your professional work attract the greatest rewards. This can be easily done in two steps. Look at the **best work types** or services that you perform for clients and the **best client segments** – the types or groupings of clients that you work best with.

Science Experiment

Best work types

Review your billable hours over the past year. This will help you identify your best areas of expertise.

- Which services earned you most money?

- Which work types earned the highest client satisfaction?

- Which client work earned you the most referrals for new clients?

- Which work types are you most geared up to provide – from an operational and resources point of view?

- Which services are least profitable and least rewarding for your practice?

Consult with your team and discuss aspects of the business that they would particularly like to concentrate on. Your clients will also provide useful insight into the areas of service that are satisfactory or require improvement. Investigate both angles and list the work types that best suit your capability, systems, expertise and resources. Developing profitable market niches is all about placing emphasis on the particular services that you would prefer to highlight and playing down the less profitable activity.

Best client segments

The same approach can be applied in the area of client segments. By reviewing the amount of billable hours, it is easy to distinguish which clients and groups of clients bring in the most income for your practice. Carefully examine the work performed for each client in terms of low input and high margin and, on the other end of the scale, high input and low margin.

Take a look at a cross-section of the work that you do for clients and find out which work types are the most valuable in terms of low input, high margin. This helps you to focus on bringing in the type of work that represents profitable income for your practice. You might also consider outsourcing or automating routine work. This strategy frees you up to concentrate more on the work that adds real value for both your clients and your practice.

Review your best clients and find out what they have in common

You may find that you do your best and most rewarding work for certain types of clients: they may be clients in certain industry sectors, certain demographic groups or people with specialist requirements. Identify those groups, and the services you provide for them, and work out why those particular clients are your 'A' clients.

It is also advisable to identify common factors in your 'D' and 'E' client group. By drawing on this information, valuable lessons may be learnt when sourcing new clients in the future.

Applied Science I have created a simple spreadsheet or table below to assist you in this process and have outlined a short example. You can adapt this **Client Commonality** chart for your particular practice. The purpose of the analysis is to identify the types of clients that you should target in the future. It is already clear that the main focus should be on targeting more 'A' and 'B' clients.

Figure 13. Client Commonality

Client rating	Client name	Work type or practice area	Client grouping /Industry segment	Annual income	Billable hours	Non-billable hours	Number of products/ Work types	Number of introduct -ions received
B	ABC Freight	Tax accounting	Import company	€25,000	250	3	3	2
A	XYZ international	International taxation	Export company	€100,000	100	10	2	7
E	Great Shop	Book-keeping	Retail	€5,000	50	30	1	0
C	Excellent Store	Accounts	Retail	€3,000	30	20	2	0

What we learn from the simple example above is that the accountancy firm that deals with these four clients does more profitable business with companies involved in importing and exporting. They are already identified as 'A' and 'B' clients.

The specialist skills in the accountancy firm are more oriented towards international trade than retail, because the two retail clients require more non-billable resources and are far less lucrative in terms of income. This suggests that this particular accountancy firm would be more successful if they built their business with a range of companies in the area of international trade in the future. While a diverse range of client types is important to a practice, a change of emphasis towards more lucrative clients would be more beneficial.

Applied Science

The actions you can take to improve your profitability include:

- **Reduce low-margin work.** Automate or outsource routine processes where possible. Some work streams represent poor value to your practice. They may be costly to administer or inefficient in terms of input of time for the amount you can charge. Look at outsourcing these work types to other providers unless they are absolutely core to your delivery.

- **Focus on high-value specialist expertise.** Look to innovation and upskilling to take on more specialist work and add more value to your client services.[17]

- **Reduce or eliminate all unnecessary overhead costs.** Review overheads and renegotiate terms with suppliers wherever you feel it is necessary.

- **Examine delivery costs to clients** – premises, systems, and efficiency of delivery. Switch to email correspondence and hold fewer meetings in return for a lower price for clients.

- **Client information.** Retain client information on your CRM system where appropriate, so that you can measure clients' long-term value to your practice.

5. Calculate the long-term value of clients

Dissatisfied customers often walk out the door, virtually unnoticed, while time, money and energy are being spent on enticing new prospects onto the client list. Yet a good client is an enormously valuable asset to you, particularly if they remain with a practice for the long term.

Consider the present value of a transaction with a good client. Then estimate the value of all transactions with that one client over their lifetime, say thirty years. A good client is always worth far more than just one or two transactions with you. It is important to consider the long-term relationship and the value that that client can bring to your practice – either through multiple deals and transactions or referrals to other clients.

The problem is that most professionals spend comparatively little on client retention or loyalty programmes. Once a transaction is completed, remarkably little energy is

---

17. David Maister, *Managing the Professional Services Firm* (Simon & Schuster, 2003)

spent maintaining a relationship with that client either to follow up on how satisfied the client was with the service, to thank them for their loyalty and their business, or

Science Fact

to find out what their present needs are, in case other services could be useful to them.

Science Theory

Customer retention or loyalty is simply the percentage of start-of-year clients that are still active at the end of the year.[18]

I mentioned earlier how Fredrick Reichheld cites the loyalty of customers, employees and investors as the critical elements of a successful business. He estimates that for most businesses, 20 to 50 percent of the company's most valuable assets disappear each year; this includes customer defections, employee resignations and investor support.[19]

Remember that first transaction again: how much you valued your new client, who you viewed as a personal win, a validation of your expertise. Every time an existing client comes to you for a particular service, treat them as if it is the first transaction. Keep that excitement, that desire to impress, that appreciation for your client in mind – and maintain focus on the value of the long-term relationship with your client. Dan Kennedy, a marketing strategist, recently estimated that for every month that you don't contact or communicate with your clients, you lose 10 percent of your influence.

To compute the potential lifetime value of a client, calculate it as the present value of the revenue that you could potentially earn from that client over a lifetime.

Loyal clients also bring in new business, and that should be factored into their overall value. Recruiting new clients costs a lot of money. Targeting new clients

Science Fact

is essential to the long-term viability of your business. However, according to market research company Bain & Co., who carried out extensive research into customer loyalty:

It costs five to ten times more to acquire new clients than it does to keep existing ones.[20]

---

18. Tim Ambler, Patrick Barwise and Chris Higson, *Market Metrics: What Should We Tell the Shareholders?* (Institute of Chartered Accountants in England and Wales, 2002)
19. Fredrick R. Reichheld, *The Loyalty Effect* (Harvard Business School Press, 1996)
20. Research by market research company Bain & Co. 2002

Once you have introduced clients into your organisation, they get to know how it works. This means that, after the first few transactions or appointments, dealing with them is much easier, and set-up costs for each new transaction or interaction are considerably lower.

Competition:
High five! Be the best in the market

5

'If you're attacking your market from multiple positions and your competition isn't, you have all the advantages, and it will show up in your increased success and income.'

Jay Abraham

On my travels, one of the things that fascinated me most about South-east Asia was the blatant and often antagonistic competition between various businesses. In the crowded markets, each vendor knew and understood their competitors in great detail: how much they charged, the comparative quality of the other vendors' goods and any added benefits that others provided that could be either copied or, preferably, bettered. In Hong Kong, one of the longest-established tailors, Sam's Tailor of Nathan Road, had to be very vigilant in retaining his clients because other less well-known tailors pretended to be him, and constantly took clients away from him.

This level of competition is replicated among professionals in the Western Hemisphere. Never has competition been as fierce as it is now between financial, legal, technical and medical practitioners. All of the people I interviewed for this book agreed that competition had become intense, particularly since 2007.

In Laos, there is an old saying, 'Same, same, but different', which sums up what competition in professional services is all about. While you and your competitors may offer broadly the same services, it is how they are presented that sets them apart. This chapter helps you to identify where you are positioned in relation to your competitors and to find ways to stand out from the others in your field.

To help illustrate how competitors can be analysed and positioned, I have created a case study of a firm specialising in family law – a family law firm. This case is based on facts drawn from a number of practices to give a broad picture of the issues experienced. The family law firm in this case has been in practice since 1941. The firm was set up by the current incumbent's father, and is about to be passed to his daughter. Unfortunately, in recent years, the once-loyal client base has declined, and this solicitor has discovered that competitors with a new approach to the market are overtaking him in recruiting new clients in the community.

The current market environment will probably remain roughly the same for a few years. The high-growth phase has come to an end, and competitors are, and will continue to be, hungry for business and aggressively seeking out new clients. Our solicitor was caught unawares by the competition because he did not monitor their progress half as closely as they monitored his. Always be conscious that your competitors know far more about the progress of competing practices in their locality than you might expect. In fact, they may even use your practice as a benchmark to compete against. Try to find out whether your competitors are doing well in the market at the moment, financially or otherwise, and why.

The family solicitor in our case study also didn't realise that his clients were being enticed by other local firms. There is every chance that existing clients of any professional practice may be courted by their competitors. Right now, your clients may receive newsletters, emails, phone calls or direct mail promotions from your competitors. It is important for you to remember that any client that you hope to do business with in the future will probably re-evaluate you against your competitors. Be up to date. Know exactly what your competitors are doing so that you can meet enquiries from clients about the advantages of your services over those offered by your competitors.

Test Case   Using the case study of the family solicitor where relevant, I have set out a brief process to help you evaluate competitors.

Case Study 3: Family Law Firm

'Our firm has been in operation since 1941, and my father built a terrific practice. I joined the practice in 1976. We specialise in family law. We always had a loyal set of clients, people who we represented from the cradle to the grave. We handled all their legal requirements: conveyancing, wills, and everything in between. This whole competition issue began when one day a long-standing client of ours called to say that she was getting a divorce and could we represent her. I said, "Of course. Let us know when you are ready to begin the paperwork." I gave her what I believed was a fair estimate. It was a straightforward case: no kids, both parties glad to go their own way.

Anyway, the client never came back to me after that call. A year later I met her and she told me she'd done her divorce papers online, over the Web, for €500, which was well below my fee. That was a client that I never expected to lose. Her grandparents were clients of my father; that's how long they go back.'

Family solicitor

It is important to find your point of difference, so that you can attract and retain clients.

Figure 14. Competitors: Five steps to being the best in the market

1. Identify your competitors

2. Know their strengths

3. Know their weaknesses

4. Position your practice against them

5. Find your place among them

In our case study, the solicitor wanted to understand more about his position in the market, because business had declined significantly, and for the first time in his career he was conscious of other players in the market, who were taking away loyal clients.

This particular solicitor had taken over the practice from his father, and the practice had effectively been in operation for almost seventy years. The time had come for him to bring in his daughter, a law graduate with ten years' experience working for an international law firm.

A loyal client base, built up over decades, sustained the practice, and marketing was never required during that time. The market changed though, and this particular solicitor's livelihood was at stake, so he decided to do some competitor analysis.

1. Identify your competitors

Our solicitor had first of all to figure out who he was competing against in his area. He identified five firms that he saw as his competitors for business. There were others, but he confined his analysis to five major ones, who were all sufficiently different that he could work out his position and take action to re-establish his reputation.

The first step was to do a **five-by-five matrix**. This matrix, detailed below, shows this family solicitor's practice evaluated against five competitors. This is how the matrix works. For ease of reference, I have labelled the five competitors in our law firm's market A, B, C, D and E.

- A is another family law firm directly competing in the same town. The practice is run by a sister and brother team who have twenty years' experience.

- B is a rapidly expanding low-cost provider that is undercutting other solicitors in the region. They are targeting a wide variety of clients in the area, including the multi-ethnic population.

- C is the online divorce website that caused our solicitor to become aware of the power of competition, and web-based legal firms.

- D is an international law firm, now targeting business in the local community to a far greater degree that they did in better economic times.

- E is a new firm, employing young, ambitious solicitors. They are operating from a bright, spacious and expensive new office in the next town. Our solicitor observed that they are networking and marketing in all of the local communities.

Each of the five competing law firms was evaluated against five distinct criteria. These are: location, people, pricing, marketing and unique selling point (USP). The USP is the one thing that makes a business or practice stand out as markedly different from all the others (see also **Chapter 6**). Here are each of those headings discussed in more detail:

Figure 15. Five essential criteria for evaluating your competitors

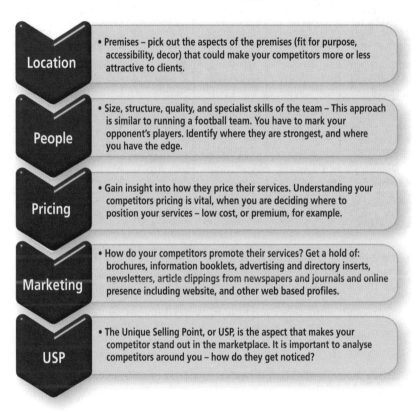

Location
• Premises – pick out the aspects of the premises (fit for purpose, accessibility, decor) that could make your competitors more or less attractive to clients.

People
• Size, structure, quality, and specialist skills of the team – This approach is similar to running a football team. You have to mark your opponent's players. Identify where they are strongest, and where you have the edge.

Pricing
• Gain insight into how they price their services. Understanding your competitors pricing is vital, when you are deciding where to position your services – low cost, or premium, for example.

Marketing
• How do your competitors promote their services? Get a hold of: brochures, information booklets, advertising and directory inserts, newsletters, article clippings from newspapers and journals and online presence including website, and other web based profiles.

USP
• The Unique Selling Point, or USP, is the aspect that makes your competitor stand out in the marketplace. It is important to analyse competitors around you – how do they get noticed?

It is essential to keep a record, whether formally or informally, of your main competitors. Competitors take many forms and can pose a significant threat to your practice. They might be direct competitors, firms or practices of a similar size and scale to yours, providing the same product and service range. Alternatively, they might be indirect competitors, offering an online alternative to the service that you provide, or operating on a smaller, or larger, scale. Or a competitor might actually take business away from you altogether by offering a service that removes the need for yours.

Here is a brief synopsis of a five-by-five matrix for each of the legal firms in our case study family solicitor's area:

Figure 16. Five-by-five competitor analysis matrix

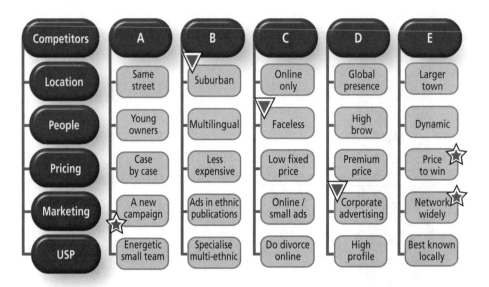

While there are many more layers that we could apply to the five-by-five competitor analysis matrix above, it does illustrate how to put together a picture of your competitors. In collating his competitor matrix, our solicitor begins to identify the types of competitor offerings, and how he could differentiate his offerings from those of his competitors, or improve on them.

2. Identify the strengths of your competitors as they relate to your practice

The attributes labelled with a star ⭐ are attributes that the family solicitor believes he could take on or replicate for his firm. He could, for example, produce a suite of client communications such as brochures, newsletters and conference events. He could also look at pricing to win business, and he could establish closer links with his local community.

There are the tangible elements, such as pricing, specialist skills, and products, and then there are the less tangible aspects of doing business. By using the five-point competitor analysis above, it is possible to identify five competitor strengths that you can adopt for your own marketing plan in the coming year. This will enable you to improve your competitiveness in your local market.

Sun Tzu once suggested that in battle you should forage on your opponents rather than use up your own resources. Therefore, exploit your competitors, build on the resources available, and use your unique selling propositions to maximum benefit. This should not prevent you from coming up with your own unique selling propositions, but it should prevent you from being caught unawares by competitors pitching for the same business as you.

In the case of our solicitor, he must build and consolidate his practice in the following areas:

- (Firm B) Multilingual capability

- (Firm D) Premium-quality suite of brochures, newsletters and relevant client information

- (Firm D) Organise and attend seminars and conferences for profile purposes

- (Firm E) Price to win business in this competitive market

- (Firm E) Network widely: establish links with local Chambers, and the community

3. Identify the weaknesses of your competitors as they relate to your practice

The attributes labelled ▼ are elements that the family solicitor doesn't wish to replicate because they do not fit with the character of his practice. He does not want to make his services available online, for example, or to become the cheapest or the most expensive service on the market. It is important to identify weaknesses in your competitors so that you can promote the positive differences between you and your competitors.

As in the above case study detailing the competitive analysis for a family law practice, our solicitor specialises in complicated family law cases; therefore, the online divorce website (C) is not competing in the same space. Yet he is now aware that he must bring in processes that enable him to deliver low-cost solutions to loyal clients for routine work. However, the larger international law firm (D) is a direct competitor. The large player is a premium-priced firm, with a reputation in the corporate and commercial arena. Our solicitor observes three weaknesses among his competitors that he can plan to take advantage of:

- (Firm C) The online divorce website only targets straightforward, uncomplicated divorce cases

- (Firm D) The larger international firm strongly adheres to a premium pricing structure. As a smaller firm with lower overheads, there is an opportunity for our solicitor to target business here.

- (Firm B) The multilingual firm also undercuts the competition to win business, but the word is that they are struggling to cover their overheads. This is a precarious position for Firm B to be in, and our solicitor will monitor their progress over time for opportunities. His aim is to price to win business, but always with an eye on his cost-to-serve and how much additional value he can add for the money he charges.

4. Position yourself against your competitors

At this stage, your market position in relation to your competitors is becoming more evident. It is also important to get an understanding of how you are perceived by the community relative to other competitors.

From the five-by-five matrix, our solicitor gains a much clearer perception of where his small practice is placed in and viewed by the local community. This information is vital in informing his marketing strategy for the coming year. He acknowledges that he will have to make changes to alter the local perception in order to build business, particularly among the younger target audience.

He definitely has to get much more involved in the local community, and he needs some marketing communication to inform clients and prospective clients about what he does. He is currently perceived as an old-style firm, but the arrival of his daughter, aged thirty, into the practice will certainly help to change that perception.

5. Differentiate your practice in the market

Science Theory One of the toughest challenges for practices is how to differentiate their services from other professionals. Professional services in general are intangible to prospective customers. You cannot give your clients a sample of your wares. Clients do not get to appreciate the level of background work that goes into the work you do, whether it is an audit, a medical examination or a case to go before the small-claims court. Clients very often only get to see the front-end report that comes from the hours of work that you do. It can therefore be difficult to differentiate what you provide to the market from the services of any other practice in your field.

My research tells me that firms are afraid to focus on one or two attributes when talking about their practice because they fear that they will alienate clients if they are not seen to provide **everything**. The problem is that if every firm aims to be everything, there is no differentiation. Logically, therefore, you have to highlight one attribute that sets you apart from the others or you will be viewed as exactly the same as them.

Applied Science

The whole concept of differentiation has been much more widely used in the business and commercial arena than in professional services. The car industry gives us a clear picture of how differentiation works. Volvo, BMW and Audi all offer a similar package to car drivers, including safety, image, performance, technological advancements and luxury. However, to stand out, each car maker has highlighted one attribute above all others, as you will see from **Figure 17** below.

Figure 17. The differentiating attributes used by car manufacturers

Car maker	Strap-line	Position in market
Volvo	Volvo. For life	Safety
BMW	Joy	Sheer driving pleasure
Audi	Vorsprung durch Technik	Advanced technology

Their chosen attribute, or their unique point of differentiation, is communicated so well that their audience knows that they do the other things well too. This is a carefully thought-out strategy by the car makers, and it makes absolute sense that each manufacturer needs to provide tangible reasons for why they stand out.

This is the end of the first part of the Five Cs marketing plan for professionals. The next part, **Create**, focuses on how to find your unique selling point, or point of differentiation.

Part II Create

Provide value for your clients to generate reputation and loyalty

6. **Differentiation:** Five ways to make your practice stand out

7. **Client Satisfaction:** The five-questions market research survey

8. **Value for Money:** Five great value propositions for clients

9. **Relationships:** Impress your clients in five seconds

10. **Service:** The five-star client experience

Differentiation:
Five ways to make your practice stand out

6

'Think.'

IBM

> *'The essence of the Purple Cow – the reason it would shine among a crowd of perfectly competent, even undeniably excellent cows – is that it would be* remarkable. *Something remarkable is worth talking about, worth paying attention to. Boring stuff quickly becomes invisible.'*
>
> **Seth Godin, *The Purple Cow***

Think of the horseless carriage, the virtual music store, and airline seats as cheap as train tickets. The most brilliant innovations come from people who are constantly challenging themselves to be better. The greatest ideas can be remarkably simple, but how do you innovate when it comes to professional services?

At a time when resources are scarce and the market is contracting, some believe that you have to be conservative, play it safe and avoid risk. Many people have said to me recently: *'We cannot afford to take risks. We have to go for the safe options. Keep our heads down.'* That is code for 'we have to innovate as little as possible'. Yet a study by the Asian Development Bank in 2010 said that China is surging forward in economic and industrial terms, particularly as the global economy begins to improve. In China, I did not observe any great urge to retrench or hold back on progress. Ireland's more recent risk-averse stance is understandable because of the market collapse of 2008. The reality is that there is a surge forward happening globally, and it is now time to prepare for positive market growth.

Top Scientist

Tom Peters, described by *The Economist* as 'the über guru of management' believes that when you approach a business strategy in this, the age of chaos, you need to completely re-imagine the world in which you operate.[21] Now is the time to reinvent your practice. This is what your big, audacious goal is all about. It is time to take a fresh look at your market and decide what you want to achieve. In a time when resources are scarce and the market is contracting, you cannot afford not to innovate.

Being different, often called your 'point of differentiation', is important because if you do not have a differentiating attribute, prospective clients cannot tell the difference between what your firm offers and the plethora of firms on the Web or in the Golden Pages all saying the same things as you, in similar language.

As you know, competition is fierce in the current market, with many practices competing for the same small pool of clients. The only way to survive and succeed in this environment is to take a more creative approach to what you offer. This part of **Client Science** shows you how to be creative in terms of your service and your overall package to clients. The next part of the book, **Communicate**, then focuses on creativity in communications. This does not require spending a fortune on altering the fabric of your practice. Instead, it simply requires you to ask how you can improve. This is about challenging constantly, and asking: how can we be even better than we are today? How can we give our clients an even more scintillating experience? What can we do today to make life better for the client? Finally, the goal is to achieve that one big, audacious objective that we discussed in **Chapter 1**.

During my research, I observed a reticence among people in professional services to break the mould, particularly when it came to marketing their services. The first concern is: how would clients react to us being different? The second is: what if no one will buy it? Creativity in areas such as accounting, law and finance can be perceived as risky. There may be a concern, as there is with all creative endeavours, of being criticised or singled out in some way. However, a creative approach based on satisfying client needs will lead to an improvement in your reputation.

If you want to be recognised as unique, you need to attract positive attention. You can only do this by being better than your competitors, having a better reputation and being more creative in how you address the needs of your clients. Creativity is not difficult; it is not even risky; in fact, it is enjoyable.

From experience and research, I have identified five areas that you can focus on to create your point of differentiation in your market. The curious thing about innovation and creativity is that it takes relatively little effort to make a noticeable difference. You will see from the examples below that this is not 'rocket science', but it can be the catalyst for great success.

---

21. Tom Peters, *Reimagine* (Dorling Kindersley, 2006)

In order to succeed, a practice has to constantly reinvent the service it offers and incorporate innovation into its approach to clients. Clients are more likely to come back to you, or continue to deal with you, if you have the best expertise and staying up to date or even ahead of the pack is an essential part of a professional's job.

Process is a vital part of an efficient organisation, as is motivating your people. We will now look at how innovation can come through your practice on a daily basis.

Figure 18. Differentiation: Five ways to make your practice stand out

1. Specialise

Many professional firms, particularly larger ones, have a tendency to offer a 'one-stop-shop' approach. That means that they provide everything that is required within a particular field – be it law, accounting or banking, for example.

There is nothing wrong with a professional practitioner actually providing the whole gambit of services that a client may require. In fact it makes sense. However, when it comes to marketing, it is difficult to make an impression on your prospective audience if you claim to provide all services to all people. How will potential clients differentiate you from all the other providers? What you need is a point of differentiation or a unique proposition that informs people of how you are different, or better than your competitors. This is where specialisation becomes important.

My advice is to be careful not to put out too generic a message. The approach, commonly referred to as 'mass market', which really says: 'we have something for everybody' may work in a monopolistic situation, but in a competitive market it is dramatically described by Philip Kotler as 'organisational suicide'.[22] The reason for this

---

22. Philip Kotler, Thomas Hayes, Paul M. Bloom, *Marketing Professional Services* (Prentice Hall Press, 2002)

is that an organisation that provides every type of service is seldom known or appreciated for doing one or two things extremely well. As a result, the reputation of the firm or practice lacks resonance. People do not consider you to be particularly good at anything – or particularly bad either. Find reasons why clients should choose you above all the other providers. They must be clear, customer-orientated and compelling reasons.

The practice that specialises and excels in a particular sphere generally gains a reputation for excellence. In other words, it works better to focus on doing a relatively small number of things very well and to be known for those capabilities.

It is said that there are 'riches in niches', and it is imperative to seek them out. Previously, I discussed how to identify the most profitable segments of your practice – the work types that you do best, and the most profitable clients that come to you. This does not mean that you have to stop offering your 'bread and butter' services: these are still very important. Specialising is about a change of emphasis. It is about becoming well-known for providing particular services or establishing your name more strongly among a particular group of clients.

In my experience, it is startling how many opportunities may be presented to you when you decide to focus your energy on a small number of specialist areas or client groups. When it comes to communicating with clients and potential clients in the marketplace, I recommend addressing a specific target audience. And this practical approach is more cost-effective. It's like sowing seeds. If you scatter seeds all over a large area, only some will thrive; those that land in the wrong place won't. Targeting lucrative clients and establishing an area of specialisation are pivotal in guaranteeing your ultimate success.

However, not all specific groupings of clients are lucrative. Choose carefully. Any specialisation that you do will require a lot of thought. Tony Ryan, founder of Ryanair, is credited with saying:

'There's a niche in the market, but is there a market in the niche?'

Do your research. Again, choose carefully and take small entry steps before you commit large amounts of money or time to a particular area.

When you target a specific sector, the audience may well be ready-made for you, and they will certainly recognise it when you address their particular needs. Make contact with the right people and look for opportunities to get in front of your audience. People who are useful in helping you to build profile in a particular niche or market segment include the heads of professional bodies, conference organisers and the editors of specialist journals. These people are familiar with their particular industry and are always looking for alliances to help them keep their audience informed. The more you know about the audience you are targeting, the more focused your marketing efforts become. The more specific you are in targeting that segment, and the better you are at servicing it, the more it enhances your reputation.

Having found a suitable niche or niches, continue to provide a regular service to clients. Simultaneously, continue to seek further market opportunities to enhance your reputation. Over time, depending on your levels of growth and profitability, you can decide whether or not to maintain both aspects of your business. Keep in mind that you have to avoid being overly reliant on one niche to sustain your business, unless you are absolutely sure that it will remain for the long term. The market is continually changing, and faster than ever before. Look at how quickly the collapse of the housing market happened, for example.

2. Innovate

Creativity is harnessing your imagination to produce new ideas. Innovation is putting those new ideas to work for you. Exercising your power to create is exciting. Whether you come up with a new sales channel (Daft.ie) or do a whole rethink of an industry (Wikipedia) or invent a new business model (JetBlue), or simply make it easier for people to do business with you (IKEA), focusing on innovation and creativity lifts you out of the ordinary. It is important, therefore, to move from ordinary to extraordinary, from business as usual to 'business unusual'. The marketing innovation consultant **Seth Godin** believes that the opposite of remarkable is not bad or lousy, but very good. Most people are delivering very good products and services in their markets. 'Very good is an everyday occurrence, hardly worth mentioning', he says. 'Remarkable' is not always about completely changing the services you offer. It can be the way you answer the phone, launch a new service or price what you offer. Getting into the habit of doing something different and better, every time you have the opportunity, is the best way to see what's working and what isn't.[23]

Innovation does not have to be overly complex. In fact, it should be kept simple. When you are looking for opportunities to create a better service for your clients, sometimes you do not have to look very far. Very often, the opportunities are right there in front of you, and all you have to do is refocus to find them. There are millions of ways to make it easier for clients to do business with you.

23. Seth Godin, *Purple Cow* (Penguin Group, 2003)

Science Experiment

When it comes to innovation, question everything and constantly ask:

- What are we doing?
- How are we doing it?
- Why are we doing it?

Applied Science

The best advice is to choose a few really great initiatives and implement them.

> When it comes to creativity, **Jack Welch** sums it up well: 'What we've learned is that if you focus on just a few initiatives and stick with them, they grow and they get a life of their own and they build. They grow like crazy!'[24]

Top Scientist

Most businesses use client satisfaction survey and reviews of competitors to tell them how they should improve their business model. While they are very useful, these elements of the traditional marketing plan do not lead to creative thinking. In his book *Managing Emerging Technologies*, George Day, Professor of Marketing at Wharton School at the University of Pennsylvania, calls incremental improvements in process, service or product **'small i'**. **'Small i'** are the innovation-led changes in thinking and the resulting process improvements that occur organically.[25] To stand out from the crowd, however, Day argues that you also have to aim to be noticeably different. You need what he calls **'Big I'** – a substantial innovation in your business.

In essence, your professional practice will need a mixture of both 'small i' and 'Big I'. Probably 90 to 95 percent of your creativity will focus on continuous improvement. However, it is also worthwhile focusing the other 5 to 10 percent of your energy on ideas for substantive innovation.[26]

---

24. Noel M. Tichy and Stratford Sherman, *Control Your Own Destiny or Someone Else Will* (Collins, 2005)

25. George S. Day, Paul J.H. Shoemaker and Robert E. Gunther, *Wharton on Managing Emerging Technologies* (John Wiley & Sons, 2000)

26. George S Day, Paul J.H. Shoemaker and Robert E. Gunther, *Wharton on Managing Emerging Technologies* (as above)

Science Theory

3. Manage process

In 1934, Joseph Schumpeter conducted a study on the elements that come together to form an innovation. He divided the components of innovation into two parts. The first part of innovation is about designing an entirely new product or service. The second involves process: how the product or service is delivered to the end user. This has important implications for your professional practice or business, as you look at how you can use innovation to improve your service to clients in that you do not have to invent a new service or product to impress clients. Making changes to how you deliver your service to clients could equally help you to differentiate yourself in your market.

Research shows that customers will pay 30 to 50 percent more for goods or services where the service quality is perceived to be excellent. Customer service is very often about process. It is about how quickly you answer the phone, how efficiently you deal with an enquiry, and how user-friendly your forms are.

Applied Science

'We made two improvements in our processes that worked well for us. The first is that we provided definite hours each day when we were available to speak on the phone. Each of our clients is aware that if they want to have a direct conversation with a member of the team, they are available at certain times, no matter what.

The second improvement is very simple. We asked: why should clients have to type up response letters to our queries or requests for information. They shouldn't have to spend time responding formally to us. So we expanded the margin of our letters and asked for handwritten responses, which saves our clients time and effort. These are just small things that make life easier for our clients.'

Accountant

4. Provide the best expertise

Clients buy your expertise. This might seem obvious. However, it is worth stating because it is so critical. One of the most interesting things that I learned from interviewing professionals for this book is that the successful ones invest a considerable amount of time and resources in maintaining their relevance to the market. Great professionals learn continually. They know the latest solutions, systems and technology.

One of the most forceful messages that came from the economic boom is that a market for a certain type of expertise might be vibrant one day and literally not there the next. Continually ask yourself: is there a need for the services that I offer or am I operating in a declining market? Has some other method of expertise overtaken my capability?

Applied Science

Dr Bríd Hendron was the first dentist in Ireland to use laser technology, and the following news extract demonstrates how her new equipment garnered publicity, particularly because it allayed customers' fear of dentists:

'Many treatments in the dentist's chair could be done without the use of a drill in the future. This is because of new advances in laser technology which are likely to become more commonly available in dental surgeries here. . . Laser uses light energy and water to carry out a wide range of dental procedures. While laser treatment may cost that little bit extra, for some the value of a trauma-free trip to the dentist is priceless.'

Source: RTÉ News, January 2010

No matter how great the relationship you have with your clients, if you do not offer a service or the expertise that they need, they will not come to you. When RTÉ announced the arrival of laser dentistry, they were also announcing the beginning of the end for traditional dentistry. While this end may take time, customer demand will inevitably define the industry. Customers who require major dentistry will in the future tend to opt for laser surgery because it is less invasive and more comfortable to endure than the old-fashioned drill. It is these advances in convenience for clients that you have to be aware of. Where clients prefer to attend meetings by webcam, or book appointments by text, or experience the latest technology when they visit you, then making it easier to do business with you may dictate the success of your practice.

A major part of your relationship with clients is to understand them as individuals, and their current and future needs.

Be timely and relevant in what you offer, otherwise clients will not come to you for solutions. If the services you offer the market do not satisfy the problems that people experience, then you may need to review your range of services.

Be up to date in what you offer. Over time, clients will tend to prefer the provider that offers a more modern service, and as a result the investment in training, technology or buying in that extra expertise may be well worth it.

5. Motivate your people

One of the most important distinguishing features of really successful professional practices is the energy and dynamism of the head of the practice. In those firms where the most senior person demonstrates commitment and drive towards innovation, improvements in client service and top-class delivery, the team, the clients and the local community tend to support him or her. Motivation of the leader and of the team is a vital part of the sustainability of the practice.

Great managers are fantastic motivators. For a start, the best leaders that I have observed are self-motivated and driven by a continuous desire to be better and to make improvements in their practice. Secondly, great leaders motivate others. They lead by example, thereby building an energetic and dynamic team, and they inspire others to be interested in making improvements for clients.

The importance of motivating your team to think innovatively cannot be underestimated. If people are asked to suggest ways to improve delivery to clients, they feel empowered and energised. Motivation works best when people are involved in a process, when they can be part of it from the initial idea stage through to implementation. All professional practitioners must relentlessly, but not recklessly, pursue opportunity.[27] The best business development opportunities are not always obvious until you do some thinking. Allocate one person to project-manage your innovation process, if you can. They will then take responsibility for the process, the priorities and the timelines for implementation.

Cost-cutting, process reviews and re-evaluation of products and services will help a business to survive in the short term. Your vision or your major objective will help you to focus on the long-term profitability of your business. Think: I'm going to survive in the short term and build now, to become exceptional in the long term. So when you are implementing your changes now, to improve this year's performance, also focus on your long-term vision and implement changes in a manner that will not have a negative impact on your future success.

Some practices hold regular brainstorming sessions, usually involving the partners of the firm, to come up with new ideas and innovations. Others involve as many of their team as possible. I suggest that involving the wider team is a good idea, because they are often closer to the day-to-day running of the practice and will have lots of ideas on how to make small but significant improvements to your service. A good practitioner will collect ideas.

---

27. "Don't Just Survive – Thrive: Leading Innovation in Good Times and Bad", 24 June 2009, Lynda M. Applegate and J. Bruce Harreld Source: http://hbswk.hbs.edu/item/6186.html

Prioritise the best ideas from the perspective of income generation, value for your clients, and the cost of implementation. Remember that implementation costs might be prohibitive for some of the best ideas, so be realistic about what you can achieve. Consider the return on investment in your new ideas. Is there a long period of time before a new system will generate a return?

Keep a record of ideas that might not work now but could provide a useful stimulus at a later date. Evaluate your ideas. Make sure that they support the big, audacious objective for your practice. Don't implement short-term ideas that might put your long-term relationships with clients at risk. Instead, harness your resources over time to create excellent value for your clients.

One person should take responsibility in the practice for ensuring that the ideas are carried to fruition. The leader may choose to appoint a project manager whose role it is to ensure that the prioritised ideas are activated within an agreed timeframe.

Applied Science

Two new specialist businesses

Here are two professional women, from different disciplines, who thought differently and found new markets for their services:

living:room Buzz

When considering selling her house in early 2008, architect Angela Carr realised she could use her skills and experience to add value by showing potential buyers the unexplored potential in her home, and the idea for **living:room** was born.

With the housing market in decline, Angela saw that many homeowners were concerned about whether their current homes could meet their long-term needs. She decided to focus on providing advice on how to help clients make the most of their homes in an economical way, whether by extending or simply re-organising the space they already had.

Angela specialises in finding innovative design solutions, working within difficult or constrained homes or sites, as well as advising on planning matters, energy efficiency and optimising space. Realising there was an information gap on home design issues from an architect's perspective, she decided to write a blog – www.livingroomblog.ie – to highlight how relatively modest changes can greatly improve the use and enjoyment of a home and spread the message that 'Good Design Works'. It is evident that living:room has identified a niche in this particular market and is maximising its potential.

Innovation Employment

After Lynda McCracken had her second child, she realised that working full-time was not as viable as it had been before she'd had children. After twelve years of working in financial services and IT, she realised that the traditional way of working, Monday to Friday, nine to five, twelve months of the year was not going to work for her.

While doing the school run she discovered a community of people in the same position: people who were looking for different kinds of working arrangements, who were accountants, lawyers, marketing directors and project managers. People who had given up work due to the pressures of balancing their home and work lives but who wanted to work in positions where they could add value – this time with hours and roles of their choosing.

At the same time, companies that she met were concerned that they had large-scale projects to be completed but, with limited resources available in-house, they needed flexible, experienced, part-time people to hit the ground running and work with them for short periods of time. This is when Innovation Employment came about.

Innovation Employment specialises in sourcing and placing highly skilled professionals in flexible working arrangements.

The environment in which we do business is made up of shark-infested, blood-red oceans, where competitors fight over a shrinking profit pool. Most practices and businesses get caught in that zone, where margins are tight and clients are over-serviced.

The real winners seek out uncontested waters – the 'blue ocean' – where there is little or no competition, and where you use innovation of such value to your clients that it makes competitors completely irrelevant.[28]

---

28. W. Chan Kim and Renee Mauborgne, *Blue Ocean Strategy* (Harvard Business School Publishing, 2005)

Client Satisfaction:
The five-questions market research survey

7

> *'The important thing is not to stop questioning.'*
>
> **Albert Einstein**

Clients do not always tell you when they are unhappy with your services. You have to put effort into finding out. Research indicates that fewer than 5 percent of clients actually complain about the service that they get. Others, whose needs aren't met to their satisfaction, just disappear into the shadows and say nothing: they live with their dissatisfaction or quietly go elsewhere.[29] Or worse, they spread the word by telling others, but not you.

While some practices might feel that their work is done after the successful completion of a particular project, a more 'tuned-in' practice will follow up with the client to determine their satisfaction levels. The benefits of this are twofold: it sends a positive message to the client and indicates a continuous drive to improve.

There are a number of ways of establishing customer satisfaction: surveys, feedback sheets, meetings, group discussion or just common sense. For those clients with whom you frequently interact, it may simply mean asking them whether they are satisfied with the service and if everything is going well: 'Is there more that I can do for you?'

For clients who you interact with less often, a **client satisfaction survey** is a useful starting point. This will help you to establish your client satisfaction rating.

When it comes to client satisfaction ratings, 85 percent is considered to be a satisfactory score. Anything less is considered to be a poor score. Ideally, service must reach satisfaction levels of over 90 percent, or the risk is that clients may find an alternative provider.

---

29. Mark Lloydbottom and David W. Cottle, *Clients4life* (Institute of Chartered Accountants of Scotland, 2008)

A mistake that many people make about market research is that it is all about the figures. In reality, it is the information that lies behind the figures that makes it valuable. For example, if you find out that 20 percent of your clients are dissatisfied with your service, that statistic is not of great value on its own. You have to understand why they are dissatisfied. You need to know:

- What are the issues that you need to address?

- Are there opportunities that you could be taking advantage of?

- How do you compare with your competitors and would your clients leave you for another provider?

- Would they recommend you to other potential clients?

- Are they planning to do their next similar transaction, instruction or appointment with you?

Science Experiment

A survey by the drinks maker Innocent

The founders of Innocent were aged twenty-six and living in London. They were working long hours, partying hard and eating what they described as unhealthy food. They had a need for healthy fast food that could be bought and consumed on the go – but they couldn't find it.

They had identified a problem, and their solution was to provide healthy food for their customers. They decided that their mission was to make it easy for people to do themselves some good. An added benefit was that the food or drink they produced would also taste good. So they came up with the idea of natural fruit crushed and bottled, so you could grab one on the way to work.

Innocent began by serving real fruit drinks from a stall at a local concert. They posted the question: '**Should we give up the day job?**' They provided two large waste disposal bins for the cartons. One said '**Yes'**, and the other said '**No'**. The answer was an overwhelming **'Yes'**.[30]

When you are doing client satisfaction surveys, be open about what you are trying to achieve and explain to clients that you want to further improve your standards and that you value their input and advice.

---

30. *Innocent: Our Stories and Some Things We've Learned* (Penguin Books, 2009)

Here are the five best ways to survey your clients:

Face-to-face interview

Ask your clients for their feedback. This works particularly well when a transaction is fresh in your client's mind. It is also a brilliant way of identifying issues that a client might otherwise not have raised. It is an opportunity to ask if you could improve your service.

Conduct an online survey

If you want a quick response from a number of respondents to a short, specific survey, then the online survey is the best method.

Online surveys tend to get a higher response rate than surveys sent out by post or conducted over the phone. Software available on the Internet allows you to set up a questionnaire in the style and format that you want. All you have to do is identify an online survey provider (one example is www.surveymonkey.com), then sign up to avail of this service. There is usually a free trial period to allow you to test it out. Set up your survey with the help of the tools supplied by the online provider. You will generally find that the tools make setting up your own survey extremely easy.

Then, once your questions are set up, you can send a link to the survey to your clients by email. The link brings your clients directly to your survey. The online survey software compiles and tabulates their responses, and you can then view results as they come in. This survey method is similar to an online poll. Best practice is to keep the questionnaire short and precise. In general, people will not spend more than ten or, at the most, fifteen minutes completing online surveys. At the same time, surveys should also be worded carefully to ensure that you get the depth of information you're looking for.

Conduct a phone survey

Compile a short list of questions and create opportunities for your client to talk openly. Then invite your client to respond to the questions as part of a routine call. Alternatively, if the questions take a substantial amount of time, book an appointment to go through the survey in detail.

A key benefit of a phone interview is that you can address your client's feedback and comments personally. There also tends to be a high response rate because clients are already familiar with who you are.

Market research company

If you are a large practice, you may want to hire a market research company to conduct a survey among a number of your clients. An experienced market research company will give you good guidance when it comes to formulating your questionnaire and distributing it to clients; they will also help you analyse the results. This method is fine if you have a market research budget, but it can be expensive for smaller practices or sole practitioners.

Focus group interview

Focus groups are often used by market research companies, advertising agencies and strategic consultants to form a discussion about a particular topic. Focus groups can yield impressive results because you can often learn a lot more about what people really think from a group discussion than from a one-to-one interview.

Formulating your survey

Overall, you may decide to do a combination of surveys. Your first survey may be conducted to discover your overall client satisfaction rating, and then a second will follow up and learn more about the findings. Whichever survey method you choose, it is best to keep the process simple.

- **The shorter the better.** Clients will only want to spend a limited amount of time filling out questionnaires, and overly complicated questions will not produce clear, workable results. Don't try to find out everything in one survey. It is better to conduct short surveys and regularly.

- **Avoid complicated open-ended questions.** Limit the number of open-ended questions. Not only is it difficult to tabulate open-ended answers, but respondents prefer to answer most questions with a check-off box.

- **Be clear and concise.** Use language that is easily understandable. Avoid jargon. If you are trying to explore interest in new service areas, make sure you clearly define those services.

- **Make it look good.** Organise your questionnaire logically and lay it out in an easy-to-follow format.

Generally, if you post your survey, it is wise to request a response within two to three weeks. If you use an online survey, you should ask for a response within one to two weeks and follow up with an email to those who have not responded before you close off the survey. Typically, a good response rate is 30 percent of total participants for an online survey and 5 percent of total participants for a posted survey. Telephone results vary depending on the relationship with the respondents.

Online surveys are automatically tabulated for you and are most efficient when it comes to analysing results. With telephone or mail surveys, you will have to set up a spreadsheet to tabulate and chart the results.

Once you have obtained the results from your survey, it is important to use them. Communicate the results to your team. It may also be appropriate to share results with your clients. A briefing to show that you listen to client comments and respond to suggestions will engage clients in a way that a marketing brochure or direct-mail piece can not.

Applied Science

'Here is a sample of five questions [see opposite] that we use for a survey of our personal customers in branches. Our objective – and it's important to have clear aims for your survey – is to ensure that our staff provide the best possible service to customers.

We can send this survey to clients in one of three ways. We can give them a copy for completion when they visit the branch. We can send them a link by email to the survey online, or we can post the survey to them. We conduct these surveys on an ongoing basis and the results help us to improve our service, and customer response times.'

Banker

Figure 19. Branch Satisfaction Survey

Please tick a box on each line to tell us how you feel about the service we provide at the branch that you visit, or contact most often.

Please enter the name of the branch you use most often.

1. How satisfied are you overall with:

	Very Satisfied	Fairly satisfied	Neither satisfied nor dissatisfied	Fairly satisfied	Very satisfied
• The overall service that you get from this bank	☐	☐	☐	☐	☐
• The branch that you visit most often	☐	☐	☐	☐	☐
• The cash machine(s) at the branch you visit most often	☐	☐	☐	☐	☐
• The telephone answering service of the branch you contact most often	☐	☐	☐	☐	☐

2. How satisfied are you that the branch staff:

	Very Satisfied	Fairly satisfied	Neither satisfied nor dissatisfied	Fairly satisfied	Very satisfied
• Treat you as an individual	☐	☐	☐	☐	☐
• Are friendly and helpful	☐	☐	☐	☐	☐
• Are knowledgeable about their products and services	☐	☐	☐	☐	☐
• Give you 100% of their attention	☐	☐	☐	☐	☐
• Efficiently process your requests and enquiries	☐	☐	☐	☐	☐

3. How satisfied are you with:

	Very Satisfied	Fairly satisfied	Neither satisfied nor dissatisfied	Fairly satisfied	Very satisfied
• The length of time you have to queue	☐	☐	☐	☐	☐
• The effort the staff make to reduce queues	☐	☐	☐	☐	☐

4. When did you last telephone your branch?

	Within Last Week	Within last month	Within last 2-3 mths	Within last 3-12 mths	Never
	☐	☐	☐	☐	☐

Who did you speak to?

	Branch Staff	Branch support team	Call centre	Other	Don't know
	☐	☐	☐	☐	☐

How satisfied are you with:

	Very Satisfied	Fairly satisfied	Neither satisfied nor dissatisfied	Fairly satisfied	Very satisfied
• Their manner when they answer the phone	☐	☐	☐	☐	☐
• How easily you can reach the person you need to speak to	☐	☐	☐	☐	☐

5. Complaints. If you had any reason to complain to your branch in the last three months, please complete this section

How did you make the complaint?	In person At branch	By letter to branch	By letter to head Office	By phone to branch	By phone to Head Office
	☐	☐	☐	☐	☐

How satisfied were you with:	Very Satisfied	Fairly satisfied	Neither satisfied nor dissatisfied	Fairly satisfied	Very satisfied
• Someone taking responsibility for sorting out your complaint	☐	☐	☐	☐	☐
• The resolution of the complaint	☐	☐	☐	☐	☐

Thank you for taking the time to complete this questionnaire.

Value for Money:
Five great value propositions for clients

8

> *'We are what we repeatedly do.*
> *Excellence, then, is not an act, but a habit.'*
>
> **Aristotle**

Value for money has become a huge issue for clients. There are clear and obvious reasons for this. In leaner times, clients are more price-conscious: they want to see tangible value for what they spend, and they tend to be more loyal to service providers who have 'looked after them' in the past. They need to fully understand one of the main things that clients require is your time and what they are getting for their money. They need time to tell you about their circumstances and their particular requirements. That is because many clients are also experiencing financial difficulties. Business clients may be experiencing problems getting paid for their services or may be going out of business. Personal clients might be confronting redundancy or getting paid considerably less than they were a year or two ago.

In most instances, clients want as much as possible for as little money as possible. There has to be concrete evidence of real value for every penny they spend. Often it is up to you to prove that you are giving maximum value for the money you charge; this requires thought and good communication. This chapter is about the five great value propositions that you can offer your clients.

Your value proposition is a critical aspect of your marketing in the current environment. This is simply the value that you provide to your clients for the money that they are prepared to give you in return. A value proposition can be described as the 'irresistible offer' that you provide to clients. What aspect of your service is irresistible to clients? This definition is simple, and yet the implementation of value is not so simple.

There are five great value propositions that can be offered to your clients. First, you need to decide what your irresistible offer actually is. The second is to examine carefully what clients need and why; then find ways to give them exactly what they want. You want your clients to become advocates of your practice. The third step is to determine your bargaining power. Flexibility is important here; you will find yourself working with your clients to provide optimum solutions. The fourth part of the process is to clearly define your pricing and billing strategy. Give nothing away for free and make sure that clients are fully informed of the value that you are giving them. The fifth is to find innovative ways to reward your clients for their loyalty to your practice.

Here in **Figure 20** is a diagram of our plan to provide clients with five great value propositions:

Figure 20. Value for money: Five ways to give value to clients

1. Value proposition
- Decide on your irresistible offer and what you can charge money for.

2. Clients' needs
- Package your sevices to suit the needs of your clients.

3. Pricing
- Define your pricing and billing strategy and give nothing away for free.

4. Negotiations
- Understand the psychology of your clients.

5. Loyalty bonus
- Find ways to reward existing clients.

1. Value proposition

If you want to come up with an irresistible offer for clients, you have to consider what value is for them.[31] When opportunities are limited, as they are today, it's very important to create value. Clients usually tell you most about what it is they want on their first meeting. Look back over the notes taken from clients at their first meetings with you. Did they tell you in detail what they were looking for? Did they explain why they chose you above your competitors?

> **Science Experiment** Work out what it is that clients really appreciate about you and your practice. What is your best calling card, your irresistible offer, your value proposition?

- **List the typical behaviours of your ideal client.** Work out why your most valued clients come to you for solutions or for a particular service, and the types of behaviours that they exhibit. How do they approach you? How responsive are they to your advice? Do they come for just one consultation, or do they have a long-standing relationship with you? Are they shopping around?

- **What are their attitudes?** Confidence, insecurity, empowerment, prejudice, concern, resentment: these are just some of the attitudes that a client might take towards a professional in practice. When they meet with you, clients may not betray negative attitudes but it is important to be aware of it, if it exists.

- **Look at clients' demands**. What additional demands over and above the services you offer are your best clients looking for? How do you meet them? What particularly impresses your clients? Is it timeliness, insight, confidence or efficiency of process, for example?

- **What solutions do your best clients require?** Identify the needs and problems to which your ideal client requires solutions. With those problems and solutions in mind, describe what you do for the client.

This type of exercise is useful in profiling your most valuable clients, and at the same time, the type of client that you are most likely to target successfully. Understanding the emotions, demands and purchasing process of an ideal client will help you to decide what your irresistible offer will be. It will help you to strip out the basic level of service that clients expect from you, and to identify what it is that makes your service special, and worth paying for. This translates into your value proposition. Focusing on what creates value for clients is incredibly powerful.[32]

---

31. Nigel Piercey, *Market-led Strategic Change* (Butterworth Heineman, 2002)
32. Nigel Piercey, *Market-led Strategic Change* (as above)

Applied Science

One of the clearest examples of a value proposition for customers is that of **Southwest Airlines**. Herb Kelleher, co-founder of Southwest, researched his client base and discovered that he was competing not just against other airlines but against the American rail service for the business of transporting passengers around the United States.

He realised that airline passengers only took internal flights when they were absolutely necessary, because they were expensive. There was no doubt, from customer feedback, that they would be prepared to fly if they could afford it. Flying tended to be faster and more convenient.

So Kelleher came up with an irresistible offer: cheap flights, no frills. He would transport passengers by air, for a lower price, by stripping out the extras and luxuries that more expensive carriers provided for free. Southwest Airlines successfully pioneered the low-cost airline model that Ryanair and other low-fare carriers have followed.

Importantly, you must create an organisation that does exactly what you say you're going to do. When you choose a value proposition as definitive as Kelleher's concept of the low-cost airline, everything you do in your practice must support and contribute to the value proposition, otherwise it will be diluted.

2. The needs of clients

The marketing of professional services is a very different process to that of selling products. The reason for this is that professional services are generally intangible, while products are tangible. Products can be packaged, advertised, their contents appraised and evaluated more easily, and a consumer can return a product if they are not satisfied with it.

The marketing of professional services relies heavily on developing relationships with potential clients. As a provider of professional services, you can only display what you offer in limited ways. For instance, legal agreements cannot be merchandised on a supermarket shelf. Nor would tax returns become more attractive in the 'reduced to clear' section of a store. As for architectural drawings, they are usually not sold from display cabinets.

At the 2009 Dublin Economic Workshop – Annual Conference held in Kenmare, Pat Ryan, director of Irish Life and Permanent, said that banks buy loans and sell deposits.

In other words, the role of the banker was not to approach personal or business customers to stimulate the demand for loans; loans should not be 'for sale'.

Marketing professional services requires a very careful balance. It has to be driven almost entirely by the needs of clients and balanced with the determination of the practitioner to succeed as a business entity.

The dilemma for professionals is how to alert potential clients to the fact that they provide services such as loans, legal services or medical services, without stimulating the market unnecessarily. One solution is to look at client 'need states'. **Need states** describe the stages that people are at along either their business or personal life-cycle. For example, a business might be in start-up mode, in a growth phase or about to be sold on. The team running the business will have entirely different requirements and expectations from their bankers, accountants and legal team at each of those three stages. Similarly, a woman who is expecting a baby will have different needs from those of an elderly woman.

The benefit of taking a need-states approach is that you can package what you offer and create value for people with well-defined needs. For example, a start-up business will require all the advice and support that relates to the early stages of running a business, including:

- setting up a new business bank account
- accessing finance
- getting advice on how to set up a business
- finding an accountant
- learning about cash-flow management, etc.

The start-up business entrepreneur has a whole range of requirements, and a banker, an accountant or a solicitor has the opportunity to create a compelling package to include advice, training, introductions, networking opportunities, as well as the usual products and services that they provide. This type of packaging strengthens relationships with clients.

'We recognised that if we can recruit start-up businesses and provide them with a good service from the beginning, then they are more likely to develop into loyal customers in the long term. So we developed an entire package specific to the needs of start-ups.

We provided useful booklets on how to start a new business. We sponsored a website with interactive support for small business owners. Members of our team gave seminars on tax relief and grants for small business. We set our start-up clients up online to make filing tax returns more efficient and cost-effective. We became known in the local area as the firm that handles start-up business, and we get a lot of new start-ups referred on to us.'

Accountant.

The same idea can be used by any profession: a doctor could create a package for pregnant women, or people with heart complaints. An architect could create a package for people who want to redesign their home. A solicitor could create a package for a person who is buying a property.

A major part of the value you can offer rests in satisfying clients' needs in a more rounded way. So instead of selling one particular service, package your services together with value-added extras to meet the needs of clients.

3. A flexible pricing strategy

Marketing is all about satisfying your clients' needs at a profit. A client is not a client unless they are prepared to pay for what you offer them. So when you begin to consider the value that you offer to clients, think about it from their perspective, not from your own. The first question is: what are your clients prepared to pay for?

Clients will not even consider your practice unless you have something to give them that they believe is of value to them. Value is defined by clients, not by you, and the most important drivers of value change dramatically over time and are different for different clients.[33]

Whichever way you look at it, clients are much more cost-conscious, and more sophisticated than ever before when it comes to negotiating price. How can you make money in this environment?

---

33. Nigel Piercey, *Market-led Strategic Change* (as above)

Manage your billable hours

My research and discussions with professionals showed that lawyers, accountants and consultants generally put in anything from 1,200 to 2,500 billable hours annually. The number of billable hours depends on the culture of the firm or organisation, the structure of the relationship teams, and the hours professionals are expected to work.[34]

I found that the average number of working hours per annum is roughly 1,600. Of those hours, practitioners devote an average of 300 hours to networking and relationship-building with clients, potential clients and collaborators. That leaves approximately 1,300 billable hours per annum.

Applied Science Being aware of how many billable hours you have per month is a good start. Then you can be strategic about how you use the hours that are available to you. Being strategic about your available hours includes:

- Scheduling those hours wisely and for the best work.

- Delegating routine work wherever possible to maximise the value of your time and expertise.

- Placing a high value on those hours from your own perspective.

- Ensuring that your clients are aware of the value they get.

- Making sure to use some of either your billable or non-billable hours for building relationships with existing clients.

Clients want more for less. How do you work with them to provide value and earn fees? Take a look at what you offer clients, with your fee structure in mind.

Look at what you offer across the whole spectrum of the price range

You may find that you can provide a higher volume of services within the lower pricing bracket, which may prove to be a useful cash generator. This works particularly well if you are a sole trader or running a small practice, but it is increasingly becoming a strategy for larger, more established firms and practices.

---

34. David Maister, *Managing the Professional Services Firm* (Simon & Schuster, 2003)

This is an example of the pricing structure for digital media packages that we have begun to offer in recent months:

A single review consultation and advisory service — below €500

Design of a basic website - 10 pages — €500 – €2,000

Digital media strategy and implementation — €2,000 plus depending on complexity of work involved

We have experienced a high demand for our initial consultation and review service, and this may result in increased demand for a full digital media strategy at a later date.

IT Consultant

This type of structure means that you have a transparent proposition at the lower level – a cash-generating proposition.

Wherever you can, discuss value and not fees

All professionals are approached because of their expertise. It is that specialist capability that clients rely on. Specialise as much as you can, so that competitors are negated by your superior capability.

In a downturn market, one accountancy firm discovered that while demand for some of their financial expertise had reduced, they had another source of income. Their HR advisory service brought in considerable business at a time when advice on how to manage redundancy programmes and voluntary severance was required by a number of their clients.

Avoid offering discounts on fees

Be ready to discuss the value that you offer your client in the first instance, as well as the resource input required to service the account. If you are forced into offering some reduction in fees, try to acquire more business or value in return for the discount. The market is so competitive that above-average fees are almost a thing of the past. It is important to charge a fair rate for the work that you do.

Once you discount, raising fees at a later date can lead to strong objections from clients.

Consider your fees to be an investment with a calculated rate of return

Work out scenarios of how much you and your services save your client in terms of time, stress and money. Sometimes clients can't quite see the value that you provide, and it has to be described to them in more detail.

Be aware of what your competitors are charging

Price wars are happening everywhere at the moment, and, in the long run, they tend not to benefit anyone except the client. It is important to be clear about your competitor's proposition, their fee structure and the value they offer.

4. The psychology of negotiation

I was fascinated by the flexibility of pricing and the aptitude for bargaining in Asia. I was so engaged by it because the psychology of it seemed to work well for both parties. The overall aim of bargaining is to achieve a win-win deal between customer and vendor. There is a level below which a vendor should not go, because the sale becomes entirely unprofitable. At the end of the barter, clients will either buy or not buy. The eventual outcome of the bargain is that the customer and the vendor are both satisfied with the agreed arrangement.

So how does this apply to you in your practice? My research for *Client Science* showed that many professionals felt obliged to reduce fees in order to win business; and as I mentioned above, it can be difficult to raise those fees again at a later date. However, most conversations indicated that the power was not evenly spread but instead was almost entirely in the hands of the clients, who demanded significantly reduced fees. Some professionals were operating at considerably lower margins – or at times no margin – on client work, in order to retain business or to keep the firm in operation. While this strategy may work in the short term, it is not a sustainable option. The next wave has to be a return to the art of negotiation, and this requires psychology.

In **Chapter 4**, we looked at the cost to serve clients. Your negotiating power is determined by your understanding of how much it costs you to service a particular client, and it is also guided by the psychology of your client. Part of your value proposition is to work out just what your bargaining power is. Your value proposition includes the fees you charge, but it also includes a host of other factors, including convenience of location, ease of doing business with you, and the fact that you have a record of the client's history and understand their particular requirements. Consider carefully which aspects of your service clients are prepared to stay with you for, and which elements they would give up for a cheaper alternative.

Looking at it from the client's perspective, they may have experienced an uncomfortable tension, referred to by psychologists as 'cognitive dissonance', when they agreed to a fee which is high relative to the value that they believe they are getting. Your role in negotiating your fee is to manage the client's cognitive dissonance so that they are clear about what you will do for them for the money you charge, and they feel that they have some input into the value they get from you.

How does this work? The **psychology of negotiation** brings together much of what I have discussed so far. It incorporates the value that you offer to clients for money, how much it costs to serve their requirements and how you gain an understanding of their needs in an empathetic way. The psychology of negotiation has five steps:

- **Cost-to-serve.** Understand your cost-to-serve so that when you are negotiating a price, you know the cut-off point below which a deal becomes unprofitable.

- **Transparency.** The greatest concern people have when buying a service is that they don't know whether they are getting value for money or not. It takes time to detail the work you do for a client on an invoice or a time sheet, but it is worthwhile. This transparency allows the client to discuss levels of work with you, and you can talk about which aspects they value and which they might have to forgo in order to retain your services. Negotiation cannot really take place unless the client understands the full extent of the work you do for them, and the input that each particular task takes. Without a forensic level of detail presented by you on what you do for the client, they may go elsewhere to negotiate a better price, without ever fully realising how much work you did for them.

- **Value for money**. Be clear about your value proposition. What makes you the best in your field – what is your 'irresistible offer'? The important thing is to articulate to clients why you are significantly better than your competitors, so that when they are weighing up your practice against others, it is clear in their minds that you are offering the best overall package.

- **Give a little.** In negotiating fees, you often find that you are doing some work – probably lower-value aspects of your role – at a lower rate. Be clear about exactly what you are giving away to clients, so that they are clear that you are willing to give a little. Where you have discounted fees, detail those discounts clearly on your invoice so that they are clear and transparent.

- **Supply a discount for future business.** You might like to build future discounts into your current business transaction, to encourage your client to remain loyal to your practice.

5. Client loyalty bonus

Remarkably few of the professionals I interviewed had any form of client loyalty scheme. This form of reward has worked for decades in the retail and airline industries, and some financial institutions also provide loyalty schemes of various types. While great work is the greatest reward a client can receive, it may not be the most memorable. Great work is expected; reward is the bonus that clients get for their loyalty.

Client loyalty schemes do not have to be formal or structured. They can be as simple as a card to say: 'Thank you for the business.' The important thing is to recognise your 'A', 'B' and 'C' clients, and to encourage them to continue to do business with you in the future.

Examples of rewards for loyalty include:

- **Client hospitality and entertainment.** Client hospitality and entertainment does not have to be overly costly; it can be a lunch, a breakfast or a ticket to a concert. Make it appropriate, fun and thoughtfully suitable to the particular client.

- **Donation to a client's favoured charity.** Again, this is a thoughtful and appropriate reward.

- **A personal approach.** Thoughtful appreciation can be as simple as a bunch of flowers or a bottle of wine to mark the successful outcome of a deal.

Applied Science

One gynaecologist always presents his patients with a bunch of flowers after they have had their baby. When you consider how little those flowers cost, relative to his fee, this is well worth doing from his point of view. His clients are invariably impressed by this gesture, and the gynaecologist gets numerous referrals as a result.

- **A voucher for future business.** As mentioned above, the voucher can be useful both for recruiting new business and for retaining existing clients. Your clients are very likely to return to you, if they have a money-off voucher for a particular service. Vouchers are easily designed as either a card, or a simple letter.

- **Education.** One of the most rewarding gifts you can give your clients is education. Run a group seminar or a one-to-one training session to help a client to learn more about their personal or business requirements. For example, training might help them to improve their chances of success, to raise their level of achievement or to reduce their costs.

Relationships:
Impress your clients in five seconds

9

*'This may sound simple, but you need to give customers
what they want, not what you think they want.
And if you do this, people will keep coming back.'*

Jon Ilhan

In the Guangxi province of China, there are several different ethnic minorities, including the Dong people, who live in the Chengyang region. When I was travelling in this part of China, we were welcomed by elderly ladies and gentlemen, nearly all of whom were bent over permanently from a lifetime of toiling in the rice fields. They welcomed us to their village and gave us Chinese tea. Above all, they gave us their time and attention. We bought dream-catchers made by the elderly ladies. Older gentlemen from the village carved our names into tablets of stone in return for a donation to their community centre. I place great value on the memories of the people we met there – the time they took to introduce us to their friends and show us the full spread of their hospitality.

The success of any professional practice or business depends hugely on the ability of the partners or employees to form sustainable relationships with clients. New clients are usually introduced by existing clients, or they are recruited through networking. New clients are brought into the fold in the same way as we were welcomed in Chengyang: through kindness, hospitality and genuine interest in people as individuals.

Relationship-building was positioned high on the agenda of all the professionals I interviewed for **Client Science**. Most enjoy relationship-building and consider it a positive aspect of their role. Most also consider relationship-building to be the most important step in acquiring and retaining new clients. Some of the people I spoke to admitted that they prefer to deliver quality work from the sanctuary of their office rather than spend time networking with clients, but they were still prepared to engage in courting clients.

These skills can be learned. Listening is at the heart of it, and as you have probably found by now in your own practice, there is no substitute for developing personal relationships and building trust over time. It has to be done.

As Christopher Locke, Rick Levine and Doc Searls suggest in *The Cluetrain Manifesto*, marketing is not a one-way propaganda campaign.[35] Marketing professional services requires a two-way flow of information between you and your clients. Building a successful practice is not just about image and promotion; it is about creating and sustaining mutual, lasting and profitable relationships. It is also about creating a client-led culture in your business. Relationship marketing works best when everyone associated with your business understands that clients are vital to the success of the practice.

However, it is not all smooth sailing when it comes to running a practice and establishing client relationships. Your clients want you at the end of the phone '24/7', and yet they are less willing to pay a lot of money for what they see as services that are very basic – or 'mandatory', as they are often called by professionals. Your clients demand loyalty and expertise, yet they are quite likely to switch to one of your competitors on a whim. You are aware that you need to focus on bringing in new clients, because some of your current client base may not be as lucrative or liquid as before, but when, where and how? You are so busy doing your job, fielding calls and managing people that prospecting for new business gets relegated to a once-a-month task, at best.

Yet successful relationship management can be simply engaging with clients on their terms by asking them empathetic questions and by listening to their real needs.

> In June 2003, a vice-chairman of J.P. Morgan sent an email to everybody who worked for him. "Take the time to call a client and tell them you love them . . . they won't forget you made the call," he wrote.[36]

While telling a client you love them may be going too far, it is vital that people in larger organisations focus most of their energy on client servicing. However, there can be internal conflict within professional organisations: power struggles, income targets and politics. How do you network, update your skills and make a profit all at the same time? Here are some straightforward guidelines to help you improve client relations fast.

---

35. Christopher Locke, Rick Levine, Doc Searls *The Cluetrain Manifesto* (Basic Books, 2001)
36. Lucy Kellaway, "Messing up the year one month at a time" *Irish Times*, 1 March 2010

Figure 21. Ways to improve client relations in five seconds

1. Clients want you to . . . listen

It may be counterintuitive, but good relationships are developed through listening, not talking.

First, it is a given that you will never deliver a satisfactory service unless you fully understand exactly what it is that your client needs from you. So the best advice is to **listen**. Remember: you have more to gain by listening than you do by talking.

Clients want your full attention. They want you to supply solutions to their unique, distinct, individual problems and needs. If you work hard at gaining a full and empathetic understanding of why your client is there in front of you, they will be far more satisfied with your service.

The problem-solving part of your brain can be so domineering that when you listen to your clients, you are only listening for problems to solve. Instead of listening for these problems, listen to the subtext, the meaning, and especially the emotion communicated under the spoken word. It is rare that people mean only what they say; there is usually more to their communication than just the words.[37]

Top Scientist Remember, also, that clients can only judge you in the short amount of time that they actually spend with you. They really don't see what goes on behind the scenes: the work, the long hours, your dedication. What they see is you and your attentiveness at these relatively short meetings. As the synopsis below of a piece of research, extracted from Malcolm Gladwell's book *Blink*, shows, those who are genuinely empathetic are more successful than those who do not demonstrate an interest in the real issues and needs of their clients.

Listening to doctors

An extract from *Blink* by **Malcolm Gladwell**

Recently, the medical researcher Wendy Levinson recorded hundreds of conversations between a group of physicians and their patients. Roughly half of the doctors had never been sued. The other half had been sued at least twice. Levinson found that just on the basis of those conversations, she could find clear differences between the two groups. The physicians who had never been sued spent more than three minutes longer with each patient than those who had been sued did (18.3 minutes versus 15 minutes).

They were more likely to make 'orienting' comments, such as 'First I'll examine you and then we will talk the problem over' or 'I will leave time for your questions' – which help patients get a sense of what the visit is supposed to accomplish and when they ought to ask questions. They were more likely to engage in active listening, saying such things as 'Go on, tell me more about that' and they were far more likely to laugh and be funny during the visit. Interestingly, there was no difference in the amount or quality of information they gave their patients; they didn't provide more details about medication or the patient's condition. The difference was entirely in *how* they talked to their patients.[38]

---

37. Belle Linda Halpern and Kathy Lubar, *Leadership Presence* (Gotham Books, 2003)
38. Malcolm Gladwell, *Blink: The Power of Thinking Without Thinking* (Penguin Books, 2006)

2. Clients experience emotion

Clients don't usually seek out professional services unless they have a particular need or a problem to be resolved. Therefore, a potential client will probably have a high degree of emotion invested in their interactions with a professional person. It is important to be conscious of this emotional aspect when meeting them. A client generally visits a doctor because of a health concern. A client might meet an accountant because they are anxious to sort out a tax liability. A client will visit a solicitor to get legal advice. These clients may not be at their best when they meet with you, and this has to be taken into account.

A personal client seeking medical, financial or legal advice is bound to be concerned – perhaps deeply worried – about the information they will get from you. While your role is to be detached and impartial, at the same time it is important to show understanding so that clients feel that they can both relate to you and trust you.

It can take time to cut through the emotions – the natural insecurities, concerns and even feelings of being threatened that clients experience when they come to you. Clients may need to be reassured by you, and they may need space and time to digest information that you present to them.

This type of emotional concern is not just experienced by personal clients. A business or corporate client who commissions work from you will also have a lot at stake. Perhaps you are a consultant providing advice in the area that they work in, and they may feel that your evaluation will expose them in some way. Executives are charged with the allocation of resources to pay for professional expertise. They are conscious when they take you on that the quality of your delivery will reflect on them and their reputation within their organisation.

It is the successful management of this emotional content by professionals that leads to the best relationships. The people who work hard to understand their clients' behaviour, and the underlying emotions that influence it, tend to form the most trusting relationships. Clients may not feel entirely comfortable when they first meet a professional. Some are worried and that is why they are there. Others experience prejudice or at least have a pre-conceived notion about dealing with a professional person. Some may have a negative perception that relates to your fees or the fact that your advice may run contrary to their own opinion. These negative emotions are to be expected in many cases. Try to mitigate negative perceptions where you can, and as soon as you can. This is done by being empathetic, sensitive and concerned about your client's personal situation.

3. Clients sometimes speak a different language to you

As stated, clients come to you because they have a need or a problem to be solved. They interpret that problem, or that particular need, entirely from their own perspective, in their own language. To take a simple example from the banking industry: a client of a bank wants to buy a home and needs money for the purchase. They go to a bank, and the banker provides them with the money to purchase the home in the form of a mortgage. The term 'mortgage' means very little to a client; it is a purely technical term, used by banks to describe their product. The way the client perceives a mortgage is that it is as 'money to buy a home'.

While clients do adapt to technical language over time, it can present a great challenge at first. By becoming familiar with your technical language, clients are entering your world. In reality, to service a client properly, you need to enter their sphere and communicate with them on their terms. This does not mean that you have to lose your technical terminology altogether. It does mean, however, that you should make the effort to communicate with clients in language that has clear meaning for them. To take our banking example, if you are a banker offering a mortgage to a client and are speaking in technical language about the 'mortgage product' and all its features and benefits, then the client may not experience a connection with you. If you talk about the ways that they can get the money to buy their new home, then the level of mutual understanding between you and your client increase considerably. Why? Because you are speaking their language.

Carefully consider all of your communication, including how you relate to clients on the phone, in discussion and in correspondence to ensure that your clients can relate to what you are saying. How you speak, what you write, what your website says about your practice or business – all of these must be clearly comprehensible to people who are not familiar with your business terminology. Remember that your job is to show that you can solve clients' problems, not baffle them with complicated language or concepts that are difficult for them to grasp.

So, whether you're providing a set of accounts or architectural plans, the language you use must be clear and unambiguous – and preferably in the same language as the client. When communicating with clients, successful professionals in the current market environment make a point of avoiding the professional jargon that they use when talking to their peers or colleagues.

Science Fact

4. Clients want a good service

Over and over again, research undertaken by the main Irish banks shows that the primary reason for customers switching banks is due to a failure in the area of customer service. Clients in general only go to the trouble of switching their personal or business current account if a major problem occurs in the quality of service provided by their existing bank. The reason why clients are more likely to stay with their bank is that switching bank current accounts takes a considerable amount of time and energy. So customers are more likely to stay with a bank that they get a good service from, even if it costs a little more. However, if the service is not good, they will go to a lot of trouble to change to a better provider.

Survey after survey shows that if the quality of the customer service is very high, clients become less price-sensitive. In fact, and as mentioned in **Chapter 6**, research shows that customers will actually pay 30 to 50 percent more for goods or services where the perceived service quality is excellent. [39]

This also applies to professional services. The quality of a relationship with a professional practitioner tends to be influenced by the level of the service provided. Your relationship with clients may be short-term, they may come to you intermittently, or they may require your services for a number of years. They are more likely to remain loyal if your service is excellent.

When a client takes up a service, they have an expectation about what they are likely to receive from you. This has significant implications for all of us. Your client may have a dramatically different perception of what they want than from what you *think* they want. If you intend to do an outstanding job for your client, it is important first of all to know what problem the client thinks you are solving. Sounds obvious? Well, it is amazing how different a client's perception of a problem can be from what you think it is.

In their book *Clients4Life*, Mark Lloydbottom and David Cottle suggest that client satisfaction only occurs when the client actually receives more than they originally expected from their service supplier.[40] Added value is the key.

---

39. Mark Lloydbottom and David W. Cottle, *Clients4life* (Institute of Chartered Accountants of Scotland, 2008)
40. Mark Lloydbottom and David W. Cottle, *Clients4life* (as above)

Lloydbottom and Cottle define client satisfaction as follows. Clients have an expectation. They expect a certain level or quality of service. Once the job is done, their perception of the level of service they received is weighed up against their expectations. The difference between the perception of what they got and the expectation of what they hoped they would get equals the quality of service. This can be expressed as the following formula:

$$Q = P - E$$

Where:

Q stands for outstanding service quality,

P is client perception, and

E is client expectation.

The important thing about this formula is that your clients tend only to get enthusiastic about your service when what is delivered exceeds their particular and individual expectations. A great part of your role is to find out what exactly their expectations are. Clients' perceptions and expectations are completely subjective and have little to do with the technical service you provide. In fact, it will have more to do with the successful interaction between you and them. The focus of your client will be on their specific problem and whether or not your solution will meet their expectations and resolve it.

5. Clients want a relationship based on trust

There is no doubt that the international economic crises over the past few years, and in particular the demise of established institutions such as Enron, Worldcom, Arthur Andersen and Lehman Brothers, has left consumers more wary of big business and major institutions. This has led to some concern in the minds of clients about whether they can trust any of the organisations that were once the bedrock the economy.

This problem is coupled with the concerns over the sustainability of businesses and institutions that have experienced financial difficulties because of the recession. Consumer trust has also been challenged by poor service offered by institutions, including inadequately staffed customer service centres, poor procedures, and apathy towards client needs in general.

Naturally, then, in addition to their normal emotional concerns, some of your clients may be looking for signs that they can trust you and your practice. People look for

Top Scientist

signs at a very basic level: will they return my calls and my emails? Will they do what they say they will do? Is this all just talk, or do they actually put time and effort into my case?

> 'Our clients' belief in our integrity is our most precious possession.'
>
> **J.P. Morgan, founder of J.P. Morgan**

So how do you engender trust in clients who may not have experienced your service or even met you before? I discovered an article recently, written on the subject of

Science Theory

trust. There was a reference to Aristotle, from his writings in *Rhetoric*. Aristotle believed that a listener's perception of trust is based on three characteristics:

- **Intelligence:** correctness of opinions or competence.

- **Character:** reliability (a factor of competence) and honesty (a measure of intention).

- **Goodwill:** favourable intentions.

People are a product of their life experiences. Some people trust much more easily than others. Those who have experienced difficult life circumstances or perhaps have bad experiences with a another service provider might be less open and require a great deal of time before they trust. Even though this is not your fault, it is something that you have to deal with and overcome.

Some clients will be open and honest about what they want from you and will talk frankly at your very first meeting. Other clients will require a number of meetings or interactions with you before they are comfortable admitting you into their confidence.

This means that you have to judge your potential client carefully when you meet them. You may need to convince them in some way of your trustworthiness. It might take time and a thoughtful approach to probe into the requirements of your client. After all, you can't do the job properly for them unless you understand what they need. You might find that you have to provide them with proof: client testimonials, references or a trial run to show that you can deliver what your client expects.

Trust, as defined by the three components **intelligence**, **character** and **goodwill** is your most important asset in building excellent client relationships:

- Clients want assurance that you are knowledgeable.

- Clients want to know that you will do what you say you will do.

- Clients want you to take their particular circumstances into account and to relate to them as people.

When you are outlining the work that you can do for a client, aim to incorporate pointers under each of the three components. Demonstrate your capability, be up-front about the scheduling and delivery aspects, and show the client a measure of understanding and goodwill. In summary, a client will feel greater trust in you if they believe in the intelligence of your communication. If they feel that you have a reliable and honest character and if you demonstrate goodwill, that shows you have favourable intentions towards them.

Many professionals focus greatly on the first component, intelligence. However, it is important to support your expert opinion with evidence of your character and your goodwill. How can this be done?

When you meet with a client, they will probably be impressed by your knowledge and your competence in getting to the root of their problem. That is an important first step in establishing trust, but it is just a seed at that point. It is the follow-up that really builds trust. If you do what you say you will do, on time, competently and reliably, then trust will develop between you and your client.

Finally, the ultimate trusting relationship happens when you add value on top of your normal service. This goodwill can take any form: a concerned follow-up call, a business lead, an information update. Think of something that will impress on your client that you are acting in their best interests, and make sure they are aware of it.

Science Experiment

Measure your trust score

You can measure the levels of trust that your clients experience with you. Measurement can be done as part of your regular market research or can be done as a stand-alone exercise.

In its simplest form, your client's trust in you can be measured using three simple questions, as outlined below. (See **Chapter 7** – on Client Satisfaction – for information on how to conduct client research.)

Here is a very simple survey question that you can use to measure your trust score.

'On a scale of 1 to 5, where 1 is poor and 5 is excellent, please rate the service that we provide to you in each of these three areas.'

You are looking for as high a score as possible:

Figure 22. A short survey question to measure your trust score according to your clients

Question: How do you rate your relationship with this practice?					
Please circle the number, where 1 is poor, 5 is excellent.					
Do you believe that we have the knowledge and experience to deliver what you require?	1	2	3	4	5
Did we deliver for you correctly, on time and within the agreed budget?	1	2	3	4	5
Did we show an appropriate level of understanding in all our dealings with you?	1	2	3	4	5

If you discover that you have a score below 5 in any of the three questions, it is important to look into the issue and discover the reasons for this reduced level of trust. Remember that your clients talk to others, and if they experience a lack of trust, they are quite likely to comment about it to other influencers. Those who experience a moderate or low level of trust are also more likely to leave your services and move to another provider.

Deal with any trust issues that you uncover immediately. You cannot leave your client's trust to chance. Your interaction with each client should rate so highly that your clients become advocates for your business.

'The Ten Commandments of Good Business'

The Ten Commandments of Good Business[41] were drafted for his staff by David Reznick, founder of Reznick Group P.C., one of America's largest accountancy firms. You will note that clients are mentioned in each and every commandment; in fact, they are at the start of every statement, because clients come first.

---

41. Mark Lloydbottom and David W. Cottle, *Clients4life* (as above)

The Ten Commandments of Good Business

1. Clients are the most important people in any business – in person, by mail, by email or by telephone.

2. Clients are not dependent on us; we are dependent on them.

3. Clients are not an interruption of our work; they are the purpose of it.

4. Clients do us a favour when they call; we are not doing them a favour by serving them.

5. Clients are a part of our business, not outsiders.

6. Clients are not cold statistics; they are flesh-and-blood human beings with feelings and emotions like our own.

7. Clients are not people to argue or match wits with. Nobody has ever won an argument with a client.

8. Clients are people who bring us their wants; it is our job to fill those wants profitably to them and to us.

9. Clients are the lifeblood of this and every business.

10. Clients are deserving of the most courteous and attentive treatment we can give them.

Service:
The five-star client experience

10

When your client walks into your premises, you want them to feel that you offer a five-star experience – an experience that expressly states: we are good at what we do, we welcome you and we appreciate that you took the time to come here. This chapter of the book is all about creating a great experience for clients and a great reputation for your practice. Here are some simple ways to get the message across that you are open for business – from the first impression of your premises right through to follow-up correspondence.

From the very moment a person encounters your business – via the web, walking by your office, listening to you present at a seminar – they are forming impressions about you and about your professional practice. Your practice sends out signals in a very similar way to a living organism that communicates all sorts of messages. These signals may be sent out intentionally or they may be unintentional; either way, people interpret those messages.

Your practice communicates your professionalism constantly as it interacts with clients, suppliers, employees and the community. The important thing is that you manage, as best you can, the image that transmits through those messages. If you want to send out a message of exclusive sophistication, then all of your interactions and communications must reflect that. If you want to attract clients in a local community setting, then ensure that your practice is visible in the community in every way possible.

This chapter focuses on how you impress clients from their first awareness through to the time when they agree to become a client and beyond. It could be argued that a client goes on a journey when they look for a professional practitioner. This is called **'The Client Journey'**. The beginning of the journey is when they discover their needs, and become aware of your services to help meet their requirements or solve a problem for them.

Many of the people that I researched for the book are very conscious of 'The Client Journey' and how they interact with clients when they first seek information, when they arrange an appointment, or when they come into the office for a visit. I asked those professionals about the most important elements involved in creating an excellent client journey. The following five points are a synopsis of their suggestions on how to create a five-star client experience.

Figure 23. Service: The five-star client experience

1. Clarity and consistency

2. Managing the iceberg effect

3. Warm, holistic impressions

4. A well thought-out meeting

5. Understanding the client journey

1. Clarity and consistency

When it comes to providing excellent service to clients, the elements that clients rate most highly, according to professionals, are clarity and consistency. Clarity means making sure that clients are fully aware of what you will do for them and fully aware of what they are to do for you. Consistency means that your follow-through on what you promise is always timely, efficient and effectively carried out.

The consequences of not being clear and consistent in your business are high. If you promise to deliver something and you don't, clients become uncertain of you and of the service that you offer. If you are not clear in explaining what you will provide to the client and what you want from the client, you risk losing the client, their payment for your services, and your reputation. There is a lot at stake.

Clarity and consistency go beyond the realm of the one-to-one client-facing relationship. It is important to build a clear and consistent image about your business in the public domain as well. Your excellence in meeting the needs of clients will be reflected by the image of your premises and your interaction with the local community.

Your team will also reflect the image of your practice. That means that everyone associated with your organisation should be briefed on your value proposition so that they can maintain that positive image for you. It is worth saying again: you want people, clients, employees and your community to be advocates for your practice.

Not only should your service display a calm and reassuring air of consistency, your employees also need to respond appropriately to clients' requirements. That may mean that you have to implement processes, service-quality training and team effort so that your practice presents a thoroughly professional face to the world – '24/7'.

Think about how you can add touches of extra value that surprise and delight the client. Consistently exceeding your clients' expectations is one way to retain their attention and their loyalty.

The following case study about ING shows how that teamwork can come together to form an innovative and delightful experience for clients, one that leads to increased business and greater customer loyalty.

Applied Science

Case Study 4: ING Direct Café

ING has an innovative retail bank branch located on 49th Street in New York City. It is not just a bank; it is also a high-quality café.

The people who staff this trendy café-style bank are also well-trained baristas who serve very good coffee. This particular ING bank branch is not like a traditional bank branch: it has no transactional capability or cash-handling facilities. All of the transactions are conducted by clients by email, phone or Web. The ING Direct Cafe New York branch is a place where people can drop by and have a cup of coffee and talk about their financial needs to people who serve excellent coffee but are also expert financial consultants.

The role of the person behind the coffee counter is to satisfy people's curiosity about mortgages and savings plans, and to explain exactly how to transact online with ING in a no-pressure environment. What better way to discuss mortgage options than over a good cup of coffee, with a person who has time to spend? The ING Café has achieved great success. The team garnered $200 million in mortgages and savings accounts in their first year after opening in Manhattan.

This concept works because ING recognised that banking had become so commoditised that only an engaging experience would expose customers to the financial services that the new branch offered. They recognised that the branch was the one place where you could do business with customers, and yet, with the availability of ATMs, phone banking and the internet, the industry was pushing people out of branches. ING created an opportunity to draw customers back to the branch again and, most importantly, to engage them in dialogue. There are now seven similar ING Cafés across the United States. [42]

2. The iceberg effect

Science Fact A key factor in considering the intangibility of professional services is that clients actually get to see very little of what you do. This is often referred to as **'the iceberg effect'**; which means that up to 90 percent of the work that a professional person performs is never witnessed by the client, but is done behind the scenes. The client only gets to see and experience a tiny proportion of the work done for them, possibly through a summary report, an update meeting or a set of plans, while you have a completely different view of the work that you do for clients. You and your team experience that job from start to finish. You deal with the minute detail, the tight deadlines, and sometimes the late nights to finish the work on time. You see it all.

Often, there is little awareness on the part of clients of the hard work that goes into delivering a job well and on time. Instead, they tend to judge you by the non-technical elements you present because they cannot easily evaluate your technical performance. This leaves clients with a dilemma. How can they judge you, your performance, and that of your team? How do they decide whether you are right for them or not? **More often than not, people get their clues about service quality from factors that are quite separate from the substance of what you do.**

42. Joseph Pine II and James H. Gilmore, "Create Economic Value with Engaging Experiences", *The Deluxe Knowledge Quarterly,* First Q. 2004

Clients judge you by whatever clues they can find to your personality, your practice and your premises. Clients judge you by what they see around them, from the neatness of your office to the quality of the coffee you serve; from the building you are in to the professionalism of your receptionist.

Management expert Tom Peters illustrates this point with the story of a passenger on a flight who spots a coffee stain on the flip-down tray. His concern is not specifically about how the cleaning service performs in that aeroplane, but he does wonder: 'If they are not able to clean up a coffee stain, are they maintaining the engines? Is this a safe plane to fly in?'

Something that appears inconsequential to you might actually mean a lot to a client, and it may send a message to that client that you aren't good enough. The problem is that if you don't provide the right space for clients to air their concerns, the stain on the flip-down tray becomes a major negative in the mind of the client and they go elsewhere. It is wise to think carefully about the image that you project when interacting with a client and aim to project as positive an ambiance as you can.

3. Warm, holistic impressions

Clients usually make decisions based on first impressions. Most people get a gut feeling about whether they will work well with someone before they have an opportunity to see whether the person is technically competent or not. New clients judge you as a person. They make the decision to deal with you based mostly on how well they feel they can relate to you.

If that requires Wellington boots for the farmer's yard, corporate attire to meet an executive, or jacket off when you encounter someone who doesn't usually wear suits, then go for it. Dress has increasingly become more casual and relaxed. The important thing is that you are dressed in a manner that fits with the level of professionalism that you want to project.

Clients expect a level of professionalism, and sloppy dress may create the impression in some clients' minds that you could be sloppy in your work. For the same reasons, keep your office desk and meeting rooms clutter-free. A chaotic environment will only convey a message to clients that you are a chaotic worker, and it may put them off dealing with you.

There is nothing like an excellent receptionist. The really great ones are efficient, welcoming and warm, although not too personal. All of the professionals I spoke to who were in a position to hire one, said that it is worth committing resources to recruiting a top-quality receptionist who will make an extra effort to interact positively with clients who visit the office. They are the people who will be the first to communicate with clients who, when they arrive, might be anxiously waiting for you to extract their teeth – or their taxes.

Potential clients may drive by, walk by, or drop in on occasion, and they will be influenced by your signage, your front door and even your front step. It is worth keeping the front of your premises in mint condition at all times.

If you are based in a particular part of town, how do you service existing or potential clients across the city? Some practitioners have a manned office in a convenient alternative location for clients to get to. While this involves the expense of setting up a sub-office, staffed part-time, it can help to retain clients who might otherwise find a more conveniently located practice.

Create a well thought-out waiting room with quality, up-to-date reading material and a suitable environment, whether your clients are children, top executives or first-time visitors getting their first impression of your business. Think of the sort of environment you would like to sit in for five minutes to an hour.

Applied Science

Keep all your guest facilities in excellent condition. People often judge restaurants and hotels by the quality of their restroom facilities. Potentially, they could judge your professionalism by the same criteria.

'We went as far as creating a five-star cloakroom facility for clients, with all the luxury aspects that you would expect in a top hotel. Top-of-the-range soap and hand towels are provided, and the facilities are always spotlessly clean.'

Accountant

4. Conducting the appointment meeting

Be timely. Manage your appointments schedule in a realistic and well-coordinated way. My doctor has never kept me waiting more than five minutes for an appointment. I can plan my day around a visit to him, knowing that I will be out in half an hour at the most. I'm actually prepared to pay more for that. It is still astonishing, though, how many professionals do not manage their diary so that clients can plan around them.

Before your client, or potential client, enters your meeting space, review as much information about their case as you possibly can. Clients generally don't want to have to explain their problem to you twice. However, once you have a basic understanding of the issue at hand, it is essential to probe until you have a full and clear knowledge of the problem that the client actually wants you to solve. That is your job.

Good-quality pens and notepads, featuring your logo, address and phone number, are useful for your client's on-the-spot note-taking, ease of reference if they have to call you later, or if your client wishes to refer other people to you.

Be clear about the duration of the appointment. Give your prospective client, and yourself, time to get to grips with the problem. If the particular problem requires more time, allocate a separate appointment or phone call for it. The most important thing is that time is given up front to enable you to establish all the facts you need so that you can do an outstanding job.

Avoid taking phone calls, attending to emails or giving way to other disruptions in the middle of client appointments. These distractions have been proven to have a highly negative impact on clients, who are usually paying for a period of time with you.

Divide your meeting into three sections. First, allocate time for small talk, which allows you to get to know the client on a personal level, and for them to get to know you. Secondly, dedicate time to the problem at hand and to gaining a full understanding of the role that is expected from you. Finally, outline the next steps, schedule a next meeting, or agree the next contact between you, if appropriate, and clearly state what you believe the client requires from you.

If you agree at the meeting that you will follow up, do so in a timely manner. Provide a client welcome pack to reinforce your credentials. Use a warm email or letter for new client engagement, particularly before formal work begins.

The old-style courtesy of walking a person to the door is highly appropriate and adds a suitable finishing touch to the meeting, as well as an opportunity for clients to reveal more about themselves.

Set aside clear, agreed times when you can be contacted by phone, provide a second contact person if you can, and make it as simple as possible for clients to interact with you.

5. Understanding the client journey

If you could start from scratch, money no object and with a blank sheet, what sort of service would you ideally provide for your clients? What solutions would you make available to them? How would you anticipate your client's every need? What could your clients expect from your practice, daily, weekly, monthly and annually? How would what you offer impact each of their five senses? How happy could this ideal make your client feel? Yes, emotions are important here: clients have got to feel the difference. What would you do to make your clients talk about your practice, and praise you to others?[43]

This section is about the physical experience of being a client. Metaphorically speaking, your client goes on a journey with you from the moment they become aware of what you do, to the time when you agree to a deal together in an office, to the final sign-off and payment stage, and even beyond that. You have the power to create an excellent route for the client. You can serve them great coffee along the way, make it easy for them to get in touch with you, send them postcards to keep them up to date, and even give them clever ideas to help them achieve more.

Along that journey, you can create great experiences that make such distinctly positive impressions that they keep the client loyal to your organisation for life. One process you can use to help you drive service quality improvements is **customer journey mapping**. This is a fascinating technique because it brings your client's story to life. It challenges you to think carefully about each and every interaction you and your practice has with the client. Those interactions are often referred to as '**touch points**'; customer journey mapping helps you identify how they meet a client's needs at any given time.

A process for client journey mapping

- List the touch points that your clients encounter with you.
- Analyse those touch points.
- Improve the interactions along the journey wherever you can.

List the touch points that your clients encounter with you

When clients, or potential clients, come into contact with your organisation, they do so via touch points. You and your practice emit hundreds of connecting signals to clients every day. Some you're conscious of, such as invoices and your phone-answering service. Others you may be unconscious of, like complaining clients, blog posts or employees talking about you outside office hours. Some of these interactions you can control, others you cannot.

---

43. Ken Hudson, *The Idea Generator* (Allen and Unwin, 2007)

The interactions you can control include:

- **Your personal approach** – your handshake, the impression you leave clients with, whether you deliver on your promises or not, your empathy

- **Your office** – location, environment, atmosphere

- **Your communications** – phone calls, a newsletter, brochures, invoices, directory inserts

- **Your online presence** – your website, and any material you make available on the web

Then there is the communication that you may not be able to control directly, but that you must influence as best you can, such as:

- **Media commentary** We have all observed, particularly in recent times, how the media can pick up a story and run with it, and how important it is to manage reputation.

- **Client comments** Dissatisfied clients are often more inclined to complain about you to others rather than to you directly. So keeping close to clients and asking them if they have questions or comments is vital.

- **Community reputation** You have a profile in your community by virtue of being there. Understand exactly what that perception is.

It is important to carefully consider the various touch points where a client can come across your organisation. These may or may not be controlled by you. For example, what people say about you in blogs may influence your client's decision, yet this information does not emanate directly from you.

Applied Science

> Touch points at a bank: ATM, customer services advisor, chequebook, website, online banking system, customer newsletter, economic updates, sponsorships, client events, phone calls, deposit receipts and bank statements are just a few.
>
> Touch points at a doctor's office: surgery sign, front door, buzzer, receptionist, waiting room, doctor's visiting room, telephone answering service, doctor's couch, prescription, receipt of payment, etc.

Analyse the touch points

Look at the type of service you provide to your clients. How would you describe it? Do you offer excellence to your clients at every opportunity? Do you anticipate their needs, aim to impress them at every turn and deliver the sort of premium service that makes clients feel great – even if they have to pay a premium price?

Or, at the other end of the spectrum, do you take a more lax approach to your clients? Do you put the onus on them to do a lot of the work? Do you stretch their stamina and leave them with the bare bones of a service? Perhaps you are cheaper to do business with than other providers, and leaner when it comes to the time you can spend with clients. Some clients are happy with that: it may suit their budget and the level of service they require.

Or perhaps you are somewhere in the middle. This middle ground is the most dangerous place to be. It leaves you quite exposed – between the premium end and the low-cost provider.

These days, clients have a higher expectation of service than ever before – and a lower tolerance for high prices. If you are in the middle ground – delivering but not delighting – your clients may be less likely to remain loyal to you. They can get this type of service anywhere: you are not remarkable.

Mapping your customer journey means tracking and describing all the experiences that your clients have as they encounter the various touch points for your service. As well as tracking the physical touch points, you should analyse exactly how the client reacts as they experience those interactions.

For example, if a particular e-banking facility is painfully slow, how does the client feel about that? What is the client's response to the experience? Do they log out before they complete the transaction? Is that aspect of the client journey losing the bank business?

Science Experiment

If a doctor's waiting room is always full of patients, how does a working mother with a sick child react to having to wait for an extended period, even though she was given a precise appointment time?

Improve the interactions along the journey

You can use the customer map strategically to make every interaction with the customer noticeably different. Remember, you are looking not just for big wins, but for small alterations in your process to make the client's interaction with you at least a bit better – and hopefully significantly better.

At its best, journey mapping can be truly transformational. Your job is to make every single step of that process a positive one – so that clients come back, recommend you and become advocates for you.

You have to make sure that all of the people engaged in your practice deliver an excellent service to clients. As the story below illustrates, if just one member of your team isn't fully clued in to your customer service ethic, it can result in severe damage to your practice, your reputation and your brand. The South African newspaper *Cape Times* on 13 June 1996 reported a story widely disseminated by the world's media, including the *New Scientist* and the *Sunday Telegraph*.

Science Fiction

Pelonomi Hospital Unplugged in Sickness and in Health

'For several months, our nurses have been baffled to find a dead patient in the same bed every Friday morning', a spokeswoman for the Pelonomi Hospital (Free State, South Africa) told reporters.

'There was no apparent cause for any of the deaths, and extensive checks on the air conditioning system, and a search for possible bacterial infection, failed to reveal any clues. However, further inquiries have now revealed the cause of these deaths. It seems that every Friday morning a cleaner would enter the ward, remove the plug that powered the patient's life support system, plug her floor polisher into the vacant socket, then go about her business. When she had finished her chores, she would plug the life support machine back in and leave, unaware that the patient was now dead. She could not, after all, hear the screams and eventual death rattle over the whirring of her polisher.

'We are sorry, and have sent a strong letter to the cleaner in question. Further, the Free State Health and Welfare Department is arranging for an electrician to fit an extra socket, so there should be no repetition of this incident. The enquiry is now closed.' [44]

The question that this article raises is: who is pulling the plug on customer service in any organisation and losing clients? Make sure that everyone involved in your practice is aware of their role in looking after the client, fostering loyalty and engendering customer satisfaction.

---

44. *Cape Times*, South Africa, 13 June 1996

Part III **Communicate**

Promote your services for your chosen market

11. Branding: Get your practice noticed in five simple steps

12. Personal Selling: Five ways to sell your story

13. Promotion: Five media you can afford to pay for

14. Public Relations: Five ways to get free publicity

15. Digital Media: Five ways to engage clients

Branding:
Get your practice noticed in five simple steps

11

'Charts leave listeners bemused. Prose remains unread. Dialogue is just too laborious and slow. Time after time, when faced with the task of persuading a group of managers or front-line staff in a large organisation to get enthusiastic about a major change, storytelling is the only thing that works.'

Stacy Blackman, Bnet, insight

In **Chapters 8** to **10** you have had the opportunity to look at value for clients, their holistic impressions of your practice, and at the market. The next natural step in the process is to communicate the value that you offer to clients and potential clients. You do not want your practice to be the world's best-kept secret, yet professionals are often shy when it comes to communicating. Inform your clients, associates, and the general public about what you offer, particularly if you have a proposition that is superior to that of your competitors.

Great communication is all about stimulating the world around you. If you communicate really well, you can inspire, you can motivate and, crucially, you can attract and retain clients. The more time you take to listen to people, to keep people informed about what you do and to interact with people in your community, the more you will get back.

Top Scientist
Part III of **Client Science** is about how to communicate so that you can achieve your big, audacious objective. It is intended to encourage you to set high standards and to be clear and consistent in the messages that you put out about your business.

In his book *On Advertising*, David Ogilvy wrote that the members of an organisation must determine what they want to **say**, and then everything they **do** should say it.[45]

---

45. Source: Kotler, Hayes and Bloom, *Marketing Professional Services* (Prentice Hall, 2002)

When you demonstrate through effective communications to the right target audience that you are an expert in a particular area or you have new ideas to contribute, you will find that people are drawn to you.

My industry experience tells me that there is an enormous variation in communication standards among professionals. That means that no matter what profession you practice, communications is one area where there is a fantastic opportunity for you to get ahead of your peers. Here is the opportunity to create an experience for your clients that is memorable and inspirational.

Science Fact

Although in some businesses it is treated as an exercise that is done in isolation, communications has to be an integrated part of your practice. The reason for this is that:

Everything your practice says, is and does communicates.[46]

All too often, organisations fail to co-ordinate their communications efforts so that they are integrated and cohesive. This results in mixed messages: a hotchpotch of communication to the market. A practice's advertising might say one thing; a client brochure might say something else; a newsletter might have a different message altogether; and none of these messages is properly supported by the employees who interface with the clients. This creates confusion in the minds of prospective clients, current clients and even employees. Great communications must be carefully orchestrated so that one coherent story comes from your organisation.

Your brand message is vital, so first of all we will look at how we can develop a profile that sets you apart from your competitors.

What is a brand?

There is a misconception about branding that it is all about logos, advertisements and promotional material, or 'collateral', as the marketing people call it. This view is too narrow. Saying that your brand consists of glossy brochures and advertisements is like saying that a personal relationship is built entirely on looks. In order to be sustainable in the long term, the relationship must value the person as a whole: their talents, their personality, their willingness to engage – and not just their appearance.

At first glance, you might think that a brand is a brochure with smart pictures and words, or an advertisement or a billboard. But those tactical items, which contain a

---

46. Kotler, Hayes and Bloom. *Marketing Professional Services* (as above)

Science
Fact

brand logo, are only a small part of the sort of branding that you need to be concerned about.

Branding originated from sheep farming. Centuries ago, shepherds experienced great difficulty in telling their sheep apart, so they branded their sheep with hot irons and, later, with coloured dyes, a practice that continues to this day.

So what does a brand mean for you? Your brand is the identity of your organisation. To a great extent, you are your own brand, because your reputation and your approach to your profession are your most powerful selling tools. The value you offer your clients for the money they spend is your brand. Branding represents the entire culture of your practice. Your people, how they interact with clients, and the work you do is your brand. Your brand is communicated through every message, correspondence or touch point that emanates from your practice.

There are **three steps to building a brand:**

1. The first is to understand your clients, their needs and, importantly, how they think.

2. The second is to build an organisation that can deliver the best and exceed expectations for the client at every stage in the customer journey.

3. The third step is to communicate to clients in a way that suits them.

The value that you offer your client is reflected in any statements that you make about your brand. Develop your brand to reflect the value you offer clients, and communicate that brand using the most appropriate media available to you.

Strong brands do not just happen; they are built over time through a deliberate management process involving strategic decisions and corresponding actions.[47] A great brand begins with dialogue. It is formulated around a promise that is made to the client; a promise that must be kept.[48]

This chapter presents the process that will help you to shape your brand. Subsequent chapters then deal with how to roll out your brand profile into the market, through promotion, PR and online or digital marketing.

---

47. Karman Kashani, 'Mastering Management', *Financial Times*, 18 December 2000
48. Robert Brunner and Stewart Emery, *Design Matters* (Prentice Hall, 2009)

Figure 24. Branding: Five steps for getting your practice noticed

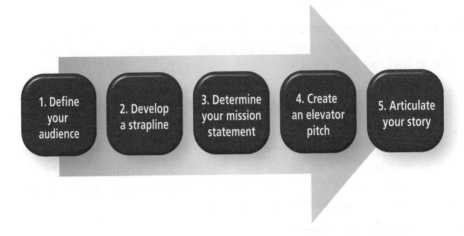

1. Define your audience

2. Develop a strapline

3. Determine your mission statement

4. Create an elevator pitch

5. Articulate your story

Top Scientist

1. Define Your Audience: who are you talking to?

In his book, *The Importance of Being Branded*,[49] John Fanning says that knowing your audience is one of the most critical aspects of building your brand:

'This may seem very obvious, but many brand owners make the mistake of defining the market in their own terms and lose sight of the fact that clients may, for their own good or not-so-good reasons, see things differently. Given the nature of branding – the fact that brands are simply collections of perceptions in people's minds – it is the client's view on what constitutes a market that counts.'[50]

In **Chapter 4**, I showed you ways to identify the types of clients that you most want to attract. Now you have to shape your organisation and your brand identity to entice those clients. Begin by choosing one or two people who represent your most attractive client types. This is your '**bulls-eye**' or ideal target client. Here's how it works:

Science Fiction

In the 2008 US presidential campaign, a man widely known as 'Joe the Plumber' unwittingly became the individual to which an entire presidential campaign was addressed. Joe the Plumber came to represent middle-class America and the needs of that massive and important segment of voters. If Joe the Plumber's needs were met,

---

49. John Fanning, *The Importance of Being Branded: An Irish Perspective* (The LIffey Press, 2006)
50. John Fanning, *The Importance of Being Branded: An Irish Perspective* (as above)

in terms of healthcare, personal and small-business taxes, and other issues, then the needs of that entire sector of the electorate market – many millions of people – would also be met. Joe the Plumber became an individual with characteristics, tastes and a frame of reference that the candidates could address specifically. The image of Joe the Plumber was used in debates and in the media by both Barack Obama and John McCain.

Good marketing makes communication real and personal. Unfortunately, individuals normally do not believe that you are talking to them directly through your communications, whether these communications are Web-based, through newsletters or by word of mouth. Most companies use a scattergun approach to address this difficulty. However, we have already discussed the problems associated with scattering seed across unprepared ground and hoping for a bumper crop. In your communications, you have to select your patch and aim all your messages at that one target audience. Then, and only then, is there some chance that your message will stick.

This way of addressing an audience works on a number of levels. It is virtually impossible to speak at a personal level to a generic audience with generic needs. If you address people specifically, in writing or by spoken word, then that is how people will perceive your communication – as being for them. You are speaking to them specifically, and they become engaged your communication.

2. Develop your strapline

Part II of **Client Science** focused on the types of clients you most want to attract – their characteristics and the value for money you offer them. Much of the book has also looked at how you can make the client experience special. Once you have identified your ideal client, and their ideal experience, it becomes easier to come up with a strapline or slogan for your practice. This will be a synopsis of what you do well, usually in less than seven words.

At this point, you may choose to employ a creative marketing company or agency to come up with a strapline; you may decide to keep things in-house and bring your team together to do some creative thinking; or you may come up with a slogan yourself. Whatever way you decide to do it, make sure that the strapline is all about clients.

The strapline should have a very clear client message, and should focus on the solutions you offer clients.[51] A good strapline is pithy, concise and memorable; it

---

51. Donal Daly and Paul O'Dea, *Select Selling* (Oak Tree Press, 2004)

realistically reflects what your practice stands for; and, importantly, makes the client feel good. Here are five highly effective straplines. Note how the message is very much focused on the customer.

President Obama	Yes we can	
ING Direct	Saving feels good	
Bord Gáis	Make the big switch	
The Sunday Times	For all you are	
Aldi	Don't change your life, change your supermarket	

3. Determine your mission statement

In **Chapter 8**, we discussed the value proposition, or the value that you offer your client for their money. A **mission statement** combines your big, audacious objective with the value that you offer to clients. The main aim of a mission statement is to make your employees, your clients and your community advocates for what you want to do.

According to David Maister, in this book, *Managing the Professional Services Firm*, the mission of most professional firms is: 'to deliver outstanding client service; to provide fulfilling careers and deliver satisfaction for our people; and to achieve financial success so we can reward ourselves and grow'.[52]

Every firm must satisfy the three goals of 'service, satisfaction and success'. It is my belief that the first of these is paramount. If you create an excellent experience for your client, then the other two – career satisfaction and financial success – come as a result.

No client will reward an organisation that is self-serving – and certainly not in the current market, where clients are more sophisticated, more demanding, more price-conscious and less loyal than before. Practice- and career-building only happens when the clients you serve are impressed by your delivery. There is no success without clients, as this mission statement from Beacon Private Hospital in Dublin reflects:

'We will provide exceptional patient care in an environment where quality, respect, caring and compassion are at the centre of all we do.'[53]

---

52. David Maister, *Managing the Professional Services Firm* (Simon & Schuster UK, 2003)
53. Ted Corcoran, *The Leadership Bus* (AuthorHouse, 2008)

Marketing works when it demonstrates, not when it asserts. This simply means that instead of telling people you are great, and listing the features and benefits of what you offer, you should show people how great you are. One accountant I spoke to summarised this concept perfectly:

Science Fiction

'My eleven-year-old son came home from school one day and said to me, "Dad, if you say you're cool, then you're not cool." That's sums up our marketing philosophy. We don't boast about what we do, or say we're good at this, or brilliant at that. We try to demonstrate how we are good by getting our clients to talk about us, or by giving an illustration of how a product or service actually works, or by simply giving an excellent service. That's the best demonstration of all.'

Accountant

Great practices think, act and speak from their clients' points of view – as do most great businesses. One of the most sophisticated companies in the world at the moment is Apple; they have mastered the art of demonstrating their values without having to boast.

Apple has values like 'design is paramount' and 'form over function'. [54] When you look at the advertisements for Apple's iPod, for example, you see that design is a feature of the product; you see that form is a critical part of the brand; and you get the distinct impression that Apple is a cool company. You notice that Apple doesn't do lists of features and benefits; and nor should you.

I have digressed a little from my original purpose of showing you how to put together a mission statement. The reason for this is that the whole concept of **'show not tell'** is the most important part of the success of your communications. Now back to your mission statement.

Describe your mission

A mission statement is a public statement about your business which incorporates your values. The mission statement captures an organisation's purpose, the value for money that is provided to the client and the business philosophy. To be effective, the mission statement must come from within the bowels of the organisation. [55]

---

54. Extract from the SmartBear Blog by author Jason Cohen, blog/asmartbear.com
55. Stephen R. Covey, *The 7 Habits of Highly Effective People* (Simon & Schuster, 1999)

Jack Welch says that most company mission statements are dull, uninspired and unhelpful. People write mission statements only to describe what they do. A good mission statement, however, describes what you are in business to do, and how you are going to succeed in doing it.[56]

What is your vision for your practice? A good mission statement takes a client-led approach: it describes your practice in terms of the solutions you offer your clients. Mission statements are best when they are succinct, jargon-free and memorable. Aim to devise a mission statement that motivates employees and clarifies your proposition for clients from their perspective. Some mission statements are short; others take more time to explain how and why they exist for clients.[57] Here are two simple examples:

KPMG. The global advisory firm whose aim is to turn knowledge into value for the benefit of its clients, its people and the community.[58]

Deloitte will become the standard of excellence by being always one step ahead.

It hardly needs to be said that your mission statement must always reflect the true value and integrity of your practice or business. Where an organisation puts out a message that does not accurately reflect what is really going on, the results can be very damaging. For example, here are the mission statements for Enron and for Madoff Investment Securities.

Enron: Respect, Integrity, Communication and Excellence.[59]

Madoff Investment Securities: In an era of faceless organisations owned by other equally faceless organisations, Bernard L. Madoff Investment Securities LLC harks back to an earlier era in the financial world: The owner's name is on the door. Clients know that Bernard Madoff has a personal interest in maintaining the unblemished record of value, fair dealing, and high ethical standards that has always been the firm's hallmark.[60]

---

56. Jack Welch, Suzy Welch, *Winning* (Harper Collins [Year?])
57. Abrahams, J., *101 Mission Statements from Top Companies* (Ten Speed Press, 2007)
58. Sigmaproject.co.uk
59. Enron website
60. Bernard L. Madoff Investment Securities LLC website

4. Create an elevator pitch

In America, they call the communication of your value proposition 'the thirty-second elevator pitch'. Every practice should have a summary sentence that describes its value proposition in simple, comprehensible language.

It is worth thinking about what you would say about your business and why clients should choose you over your competitors. In an 'elevator pitch', you have twenty-five words – or approximately thirty seconds – to make your point. In **Chapter 8**, we spent time looking at the value proposition, or the irresistible offer that you have for clients. When it comes to communicating your value proposition, it follows the same principle as a chat-up line. Very often, you only have a short time to provide a potential client with a summary of why they should choose you above your competitors.

This communication should be convincing and memorable, and should demonstrate why you are better, rather than assert that you are better. So while you might be tempted to say: 'We're number one in the market' – that really says little about what you can do for the client, and is not really a compelling proposition.

The people behind Innocent – the smoothie company – translate the real meaning of their business into easily understood language. Here's their description of what a value proposition should say:

'The world of commerce rewards simplicity and its associates, clarity and focus. So it's always worth applying the granny test: in other words, you should be able to explain your business idea and how it will beat the competition in a simple sentence that your granny would understand.' [61]

People make the mistake of telling potential clients that they are fantastic at what they do, without offering the evidence to prove it. So in your pitch for new business, don't brag and boast, don't show structure charts and titles – they are only relevant internally. Instead, show that you understand the problems or needs that the client has, and how you can solve those problems. Demonstrate also the 'feel-good' factor of dealing with you. This is most successfully demonstrated to potential clients through existing customer case studies, client testimonials, and quotes from existing clients that explain how you add value.

When it comes to client communications, the most important word is 'credibility'. We are living in an age where the trust, credibility and authenticity of professionals are often called into question. Your communications have to convey a message of

---

61. *Innocent: Our Stories and Some Things We've Learned* (Penguin Books, 2009)

credibility and genuineness, and it must be clearly understood by your audience. Over-promising does not work. Boasting is not appreciated. Bold statements about how great you are tend not to be of interest to a potential client.

Clients are interested in examples of how the value that you offer will apply to their specific needs. Your brand should convey your capability and the excellence of your service through your examples, through client endorsements, and through case studies that clearly demonstrate how your services can be delivered in practice.

5. Articulate your story

There is an interesting revival taking place among the global business community. CEOs and their strategists who are looking to achieve visibility over competitors, to generate greater loyalty from existing clients, to motivate employees, and to develop a positive profile generally are looking to the ancient art of **storytelling**.

Every business has its own story – its own history, if you like – because behind every business story, there are people. For a number of years, particularly during the boom years, the story of the people involved in organisations was partially lost among profit figures, share prices and market-share data. Suddenly, in a time of negative to moderate growth, and in a tougher competitive climate, the stories, the human interest angle and the original credentials of your practice could make your practice into the irresistible offer that we mentioned in **Chapter 8**.

Why is your story important? A story is an omnipresent form of communication because people relate to stories far more comfortably than they do to figures or buildings or brochures. Stories tend to be our most memorable, most charismatic form of communication. That explains why soap operas are so popular (in fact, soap operas were originally invented to sell soap powder).

While clients are primarily interested in how you can help solve their problems or satisfy their needs at a given time, your story, the tradition of your practice, and the values that you stand for can help to demonstrate to clients that you are good at what you do, that you are personally involved and interested in the profession that you practice, and that you are empathetic as a human being. You have your story too.

Science Fact

Clients want you to do a good job, but you will stay in their memory through the emotive connection that binds people as individuals.

All of this might sound a bit 'touchy-feely', but it is important in terms of your communication with your clients. Most clients are unlikely to have an analytical interest in your business. Instead, most prefer to connect with you personally and with the values of your organisation. Your story can put you and your practice into a frame that is easily understood and appreciated. Your story may help people develop a clearer understanding of who they are dealing with and the type of practice you run.

There are interesting ways to use stories to convey the values of your business. Whether you want to demonstrate your operational excellence, the dedication of your employees, or the solutions-focused nature of your practice, a story can be used to great effect. There are parables that give examples of moral fortitude, survival stories that paint a picture of resilience, and motivational stories that make people want to jump into action.

Top
Scientist

A fascinating example of how stories work to help market people is how Barack Obama managed to project himself so that he would rise from his position as a relatively unknown Senator to make history by becoming America's first African-American president. He achieved this through an extremely well-planned campaign that harnessed his personal story, his openness and his superb interpersonal skills.

The interesting thing about Barack Obama is that he uses a very personal approach to win widespread support. President Obama appears to have developed a powerful one-to-one relationship with most of an entire nation. How did he achieve this?

The answer is that he told his story and took on board the stories of the American people. Obama communicated the story of who he is, his background, and his personal struggles in an open, warm and honest way. He, in turn, listened to people's stories, their concerns, their struggles, and reflected his understanding and empathy for their issues in his campaign.

Once you have found your story, how do you communicate it? Again, we can use the example of how President Obama managed to communicate his story to 'woo' the world.

Obama used small networking gatherings so that people could get to know the 'real' Barack Obama. He orchestrated huge rallies to communicate his understanding of what he had heard and learned to a greater proportion of the voting population. He used online social networking to appeal to young adults – a largely untapped segment of the electorate. He even profiled his full personal history online, on his website, on FaceBook, and through a variety of other social media – something that no other presidential candidate had done before. Obama summarised his campaign by saying:

'What began as a whisper has swelled into a chorus we cannot ignore. Yes we can.'

Take a look at President Obama's FaceBook page, on which he tells you that his favourite movies are *Casablanca* and *The Godfather I* and *The Godfather II*. His favourite musicians and composers include Miles Davis, John Coltrane, Bob Dylan, Stevie Wonder, Johann Sebastian Bach and The Fugees. One of his favourite books is *Moby Dick*.[62]

Obama is not afraid to share something of himself in order to gain the trust and understanding of others. This sharing leads to greater levels of trust from those he meets. Wherever he goes, people are prepared to open up to him, and there are many in America who believe that they have a personal connection with Obama because he is prepared to share a significant part of who he is.

Who in the world could not relate to Barack Obama's story? It fosters trust and openness. It made voters think: if this guy is so open about his own history, he must be open in his political dealings. Obama was convinced of the importance of his personal story to his winning of the presidential race, as this comment to a journalist illustrates:

'If the American people know me and my story and Michelle, then I think we'll win.'

As president, Barack Obama continues to nurture the relationship he began with American voters by creating opportunities for open discourse, reflection and feedback. Think also of the positive impact that his interactive style is having on the world. And critically, at the same time, Obama has not lost his solidly professional image.

Summary

Science Fact

● **Your brand is your practice; your practice is your brand.**

Your brand, your strapline, your mission, your story – all of these elements must be supported by the actions of your practice or they hold no weight whatsoever. A powerful brand name, or strapline, or mission statement, is useless without the actions to prove what you say you can do. When you set up in practice to offer a service to clients, it's not about the words you use, it's about the actions you deliver for the client. You have to show clients that you are excellent in your delivery, and it is this delivery that most effectively supports a great brand.

---

62. www.facebook.com/barackobama

How to communicate your brand

Modern communications techniques have not been widely used by professional firms, but in more competitive times it makes sense to build a recognisable brand using every form of media available to you.

So how does your business communicate to the outside world? Communication is every message your business sends out to the world: every letter, every invoice, your website, your emails, telephone contact, business contracts, supplier engagements, bill payments, the premises you operate from, and your answering service. Your business never stops communicating.

Taking full ownership of all that communication is vital for the success of your practice. The person who owns the communications for your practice is not the one who produced your website, or the person who drafts the contracts, or the one who prints your brochures. The owner of the communication is the person who depends ultimately on the success or failure of that communication: that is, you.

The various elements of communications for a practice should be as **integrated** as possible. By integrated, I mean that they should have a common design style, a common message about your practice, a common appearance and a common tone of voice.

Types of marketing communications

There are a wide variety of communication tools that you can use to tell the story of your brand. From my experience in marketing, I have chosen four areas that directly relate to professionals in practice. Again, I have drawn on my interviews with a wide range of professional people.

Originally, marketing communications was designed to sell consumer products and services rather than professional services, which are less tangible. However, as discussed in the introduction, professionals are increasingly using the whole spectrum of communications tools as a way of attracting new clients.

The next four chapters are designed to give you marketing communications ideas, from how to do personal selling through to running promotions such as advertising and conferences, to approaching journalists and using modern technology to market your business or practice.

Figure 25. Using the media to promote your brand

Personal Selling - Five opportunities to sell your story	Promotion - Five media you can afford to pay for	PR - Five angles to attract free publicity	Digital Media - Five ways to engage clients
Introductions	Advertising	Help a journalist	Cloud computing
Sales pitch	Direct marketing	Supply topical stories	Website
Networking	Conferences and seminars	Write for industry journals	LinkedIn
Sales meetings	Sponsorships	Hold a press launch	Blogging
Pitch books and tender documents	Promotional items	Publicise an award	YouTube

Once you have established your brand – and an image with which to publicise that brand – how do you go about using your brand to recruit clients and to hold on to the clients you already have? In the remaining chapters of this part about **Communication**, we will first look at the distinct communication channels you can use to generate publicity and attract new clients. And it is important to note that these communications channels are also useful for reinforcing your existing client's loyalty to your business and for keeping your key influencers and collaborators on-side.

What are the elements that make a brand great?

- **Be real** – Be realistic about your clients, their needs and how you address them.

- **Tell the story** – Your brand is the story of how you have created an organisation to fulfil the needs of your clients. Your story deals with your values in a way that will make the brand real and memorable.

- **Evolve continuously** – Develop new ideas, new services, new ways of making your clients happy.

- **Consistent image** – Create a consistent and professional look, feel and tone across all of your communications to clients, collaborators and employees.

- **Involve clients** – Make your brand a journey of discovery for you and your clients together. Look for their insight and show them how you respond to their ideas.

- **Lead the market** – Seek to bring cutting-edge technology, ideas, services and quality of service to your clients wherever you can.

- **Innovate** – Wherever you can, find ways to make it better, easier, and more rewarding for clients to do business with you. This requires creative thinking, but it is well worth it.

- **Attitude** – Reflect the attitude of your customers where this is positive and can-do. Also, develop the kind of compelling attitude that exudes collaboration, success and innovation.

- **Demonstrate integrity** – Now more than ever, it is vital to find ways to actively demonstrate authenticity, integrity, fairness and transparency.

- **Core values** – Maintain close connection with the values that you have identified that make you stand out as being different.

- **Client call** – The type of customers that you take on strongly influences your brand.

- **Passion** – Nothing sells like passion. If you deeply believe in the power of what you offer, and you have the confidence to convey the benefits to clients, you will win.

- **Client perception** – If clients perceive that the value you present has benefits for them, that's a brand. If your value proposition is outmoded, then so is your brand.

Personal Selling:
Five ways to sell your story

12

> 'You can have brilliant ideas, but if you
> cannot get them across, your ideas will not get you anywhere.'
>
> **Lee Iacocca**

When the market weakened in the late 'noughties', new business referrals from existing clients, family and friends became less frequent. This has left many professionals in a difficult position. Some of the people I spoke to said that they had never had to engage before in any formal activity to generate new leads or introductions, but that because of the downturn in the market, they were going to have to do this in order to sustain their business.

Competition in the banking industry increased significantly in the 1990s, and, as a result, the focus of banking changed from administration and management to sales. This represented a huge cultural change for bankers and the banking industry: where once new customers went to their local bank to ask for a current account, a savings plan or a mortgage, now bankers had to engage in selling to potential clients in a very competitive market. Some people took to sales with great energy, while others found it extremely difficult to adapt from reading balance sheets and administering accounts to knocking on doors looking for business. And the reality is that, over the past decade, some other professionals had to follow the path that bankers took towards a more sales-focused approach and others did not. My research indicates to me that a great proportion of professional practitioners are considering some form of sales activity in the current environment.

The personal approach is the most important form of relationship communications for professionals is the personal approach. While the term '**personal selling**' may not be one that professionals would choose to describe what they do to win business, I believe that all of your dealings with clients and prospective clients involve personal selling. In Part II of the book we examined how clients obtain a holistic impression of you and your practice, and about how you have to be conscious of your role in relating to and empathising with clients. Creating this good impression involves selling yourself and your practice.

The key to this is to decide what impression you want to create and to build all of your communications, and your sales approach, to make sure that clients get the message clearly about what you stand for, who you are as a person, and what makes your practice stand out as better than your competitors.

There is no doubt that your professionalism requires you to take a more subtle and relationship-oriented approach, rather than one of the 'hard sell'. At the same time, many of you find that you have to network more, and find new clients in an altogether different way.

Figure 26. Personal Selling: Five ways to sell your story

1. Introductions

I asked everyone I interviewed for **Client Science** which method was the best way to attract new clients. They all agreed that, until recently, word-of-mouth was the single best way to get new clients. If a client is happy with you, they are very likely to tell someone else about how good you are, and the message spreads. (The reverse is also true too, of course.)

> 'I rely solely on word-of-mouth. One client refers another. No advertising, no directories, no website.'
> **Sole-practitioner accountant**

Most people agreed that a referral from an existing client is the best form of new business development. Your client's great experience with you becomes a story to tell contacts, friends and family. Up to now, these word-of-mouth referrals were generally unsolicited or unprompted. A new client, referred by an existing client, simply rang up or called in, and your business grew exponentially as a result.

The market has altered, however, and so have the dynamics of acquiring new referrals. Like the bankers in the 1990s, clients no longer simply arrive at your door: you have to go out and find them.

> 'If you decide you want to get business, then you can and you will. Ask your customers and your neighbours out in the community to introduce you to new contacts. Get an introduction, not a referral. You don't ask someone to refer business; you ask a person to introduce you to someone who they think might like to do business with you.'
> **Banker**

A referral is simply a name that you can follow up, whereas an introduction is someone who is personally introduced to you; the latter is a far stronger lead.

How do you get more introductions? The simple answer is to **ask**. Call or write to your existing clients to ask them for introductions. Attach a brief note to your email signature asking for introductions to new clients. Talk to colleagues, friends and relations, and ask them to introduce you to prospective clients if they can. Here is a note that one person used on their email signature:

'If you are satisfied with my service and if you know someone who could benefit from what I provide, please introduce me to them. I would be delighted to meet them.'

Introductions to new clients don't just come from existing clients. Sometimes you just have to network to meet new people and make a sales pitch to attract their attention.

Applied Science

Like many other international business chambers, the Dublin Chamber of Commerce holds regular networking evenings, called 'Network and Get Work'. These evenings are run like 'speed-dating' events. Participants are invited to attend networking evenings in a large room, and they are supplied with light refreshments. Attendees are encouraged to network with, explain their business to, and swap business cards with as many other people as possible. Attendance at these networking events went up 200 percent in 2009 as people in all types of industries responded to the need to generate more contacts and more business.

2. Sales pitch

A well-crafted sales pitch brings together all that is great about your practice. The pitch is about making an impression on a potential client so that you can move to the next level – that is, to get their agreement to avail of your services. It is all about how you gain an understanding of clients' needs: your desire to ask questions and empathetically listen to a person who needs a solution; the service you can provide; your experience; your ability to come up with a specialised and customised idea that meets their individual needs. Your sales pitch is a summary of what you can do. If it is well-crafted, your explanation of the solutions you can provide will fit perfectly with what your potential client wants from you.

Remember to keep the content of your value proposition, your mission statement and your thirty-second elevator pitch in front of you. Your ultimate aim is to convey your supreme interest in your clients, the superior value that you offer, and fundamental messages about your organisation.

There is no doubt that a one-to-one meeting is the best environment for making your sales pitch and negotiating the first stages of a mutual working arrangement. However, you do not always have the luxury of a one-to-one situation. When you are out networking at events, you may have to deliver your sales pitch very quickly, in a crowded room, to complete strangers. For all types of professionals, this is an extremely challenging way of developing business, and few really enjoy it. However, if it means the difference between finding new clients quickly and not having enough clients, networking may be an essential part of the development of your practice.

3. Networking

Once you get in front of a prospective client, whether at a networking event, over a cup of coffee or in a group-meeting scenario, the process of personal selling begins. According to an article by Stephen Brown in the *Harvard Business Review on Marketing*: 'People still enjoy the iconic art of the well-crafted sales pitch.'[63]

The other thing to bear in mind is that networking in groups is not really that difficult. Networking is about chatting to people, listening, and having a good 'chat-up line' about you and your practice. That chat-up line is your thirty-second elevator pitch, which was outlined in the last chapter. You have the tools; now you can get on to the networking phase.

How to handle a networking opportunity

Listening is a vital skill when it comes to networking. Ask questions, probe and listen. A person you meet at a networking event, seminar or conference might reveal an issue or a problem that you can resolve for them at a later date. They may be able to introduce you to prospective clients. They may be useful 'link people' in your networking group.

At a networking event, if someone approaches you and asks 'What do you do?', you are missing a big opportunity if you just reply that you are a solicitor or a doctor or an accountant. Respond with a phrase that prompts the other person to ask for more information. (We will examine in more detail how to talk about your business in later chapters.)

Explain what you do by stating how you help your clients. For example, you might say: 'I work with businesses to help them understand how they can significantly reduce costs.' The natural response to that is 'How do you do that?' This stimulates further conversation – and presents an opportunity for you to explain who you are and what you do in more detail. If there is no response, the person you are talking to is probably not a prospective client, and you should move on to the next person and begin the process again.[64]

---

63. Stephen Brown, "Torment your customers (They'll Love it)" (*Harvard Business Review*, Vol. 79, No. 9, October 2001.)
64. Mark Powers and Shawn McNalis, *How Good Attorneys Become Great Rainmakers* (Independently published, 2009)

You must then pose the question 'What do *you* do?' Enjoy the two-way flow of the networking process. Ask questions that show that you are interested in the potential client's business. Give examples that illustrate how you work.

Seán Weafer is an international expert on creating 'high trust advisors, leaders and teams'. He provides some useful advice on networking to get work:

Five steps to help you get speaking to the right person

Choose the correct event

Select the event which is most suited to your particular profession and to that of your prospective clients. For business-to-business networking, the best place to meet clients may be at their own industry conferences.

Target the people you want to meet.

It is wise to be selective, if you possibly can. Choose the people you want to meet. Usually you can get hold of a delegate list from the conference organisers beforehand. Research the people you list as targets, so that you can show some knowledge of their business interests when you meet them. Have a target of at least three people per event.

Learn the psychology of networking

Conferences and seminars are not just a mass of people, even though they can sometimes appear that way. If you look around you, you will observe that people are usually arranged in three distinct ways:

Individuals – looking to talk to people, seeking a way in, probably with the objective of networking, just like you. Generally, these individuals will welcome the opportunity to talk to you and may even see you as a lifeline. Not a bad start.

The open group – this is a small group of individuals who have gathered together for networking purposes. Chances are they don't know each other well and their body language tells you that they are open to more people entering the group. Join a mixed-gender group, if this is an option.

The closed group – this group is physically arranged so that there is little or no room to join in. They know each other, or at the very least are engaged in deep conversation. There is no point in attempting to break the discussion by entering this group: they are closed to discussion – for the time being anyway.

Making the approach

How do you get talking to people? Common courtesy, actually. Make your approach to either an individual or an open group.

Make eye contact and smile.

Request permission to join them. 'Do you mind if I join you?'

Wait for a response. It is generally positive – after all, that's why people are there.

Extend your hand to shake hands.

Join the group.

Ask questions and actively listen

To be interesting to people, you should first be interested in them. The best way to build a relationship in the beginning is to ask neutral and open questions, such as: 'What's your connection with the event?' and 'Are you here as a delegate or a speaker?'

Neutral questions cause people to relax because they come across as non-threatening. They give you and the other person time to establish rapport. Then you can move on to professional matters. Ask them questions about their business interests, their profession and their current suppliers.

Do not attempt to market yourself at this time. The initial discussion leads up to an exchange of business cards, and you can then ask permission to make a contact call and arrange to meet at a later date.

Source: Seán Weafer, from the articles: "R'evolutionary Networking Part 1 & 2" on his website www.seanweafer.com

4. Sales meeting

You get an introduction to a potential client who would now like to meet you to talk about what you can do for them. Your introduction may have come from an existing client, from a networking evening or from one of your various contacts. Now you have to present either at a one-to-one meeting or in at a formal group meeting. What do you do?

Applied Science

Most of the professionals I spoke to are comfortable with their performance at this stage of the process.

> 'Once I get a client in front of me, in this office, then invariably I win their business. I am confident that we provide the best service around, and it is just a matter of convincing the client that we are the best.'   **Accountant**

It is worth covering a few points on how to handle a sales meeting: competition is so intense that one cannot afford to miss an opportunity.

Five things you should consider before your sales meeting

- Preparation prior to your meeting is critical. The old adage: 'fail to plan, plan to fail', is true. As part of your pre-planning:
  o set meeting objectives,
  o know who you are meeting,
  o research the people and their business on the Internet, and
  o set an agenda for the meeting.

- The initial greeting and introductions are more important than you may think. People make instantaneous judgements about who you are based on your handshake and your greeting.
  o Make sure that you give a warm professional greeting.
  o Let everyone at the meeting introduce themselves.

- Listen. Listen. Listen.
  o We have two ears and one mouth. We should use them in that proportion.
  o It shows great respect to listen to a client and discuss their business.
  o Use case studies, references to other clients and testimonials to show you understand their requirements.

- Find out what the needs are of the people at the meeting as they relate to you:
  o What are their issues or problems?
  o How can you solve them?
  o Is it the decision-maker you are meeting? Do they control the budget?

- Follow up.
  o Agree next steps at the end of the meeting
  o Follow up on any agreed actions in a prompt manner.

Source: Fiona Flynn, Sales Solutions

5. Pitch book and tender documents

A pitch for business can be a short letter, a PowerPoint presentation or a longer tender document. While pitch letters and presentations tend to be in response to a query about what you can do, tenders are more formal documents with specific questions requiring detailed answers.

The most important aspect of a pitch or a tender document is to make sure that there is a **full understanding of what the prospective client is looking for**. What are their needs and problems, and what role do they expect you to play to provide a solution?

A number of people that I interviewed for **Client Science** said that they are careful about how many pitch or tender documents they take on. These documents often require hours of detailed input, and in the end the client may use them to help them understand the market or to manage their existing suppliers better.

> 'We prefer, if possible, to meet the person or an individual from the organisation that requests a tender from us. Then we talk through what we offer, get a more in-depth view of what the client is really looking for, and sometimes we get insight that says that the person does not really want our services at all. Part of the research at this stage is to find out if people are prepared to pay what we charge for our design work and implementation.'
>
> **Website developer**

Your pitch for business may involve a presentation to an individual or a team of people. In any case, your content is crucial to the success of the pitch: it should not be generic. I have seen hundreds of generic pitches – presentations made up for any audience and not tailored to the specific needs of the person being addressed. Those kinds of pitches lose their audience's attention instantly.

The pitch that works best is one that takes the understanding that you gain about what the potential client is really contending with, and incorporates this into the presentation, so that at every opportunity, their needs are specifically referred to. This type of pitch is much more relevant and satisfying to deliver, and far more appealing and relevant to your audience.

Steer clear of long-winded descriptions of your practice, numbers of people, square footage of premises, and organisation charts. Those details are best kept for the internal review and restructure presentations. Focus on how your practice will structure itself to meet the requirements of the client. Marketing really works when it shows, rather than boasts about, what the business or practice can do. Use relevant examples to show how you handled a similar issue before. Use client testimonials to illustrate how a service worked and how you satisfied the client's needs or resolved their problems. Use clear process charts to show how your client's organisation can interact with your organisation to ensure a smooth transition and delivery of the service.

Top Scientist Avoid telling clients that you are the best – because they will require proof. On the other hand, in your pitch, mention awards that you have you won, positive publicity, and compliments from clients.

As professionals, many of you are expert public speakers, but for those who need guidance, here are five pointers about how to frame a pitch, presentation or speech

Applied Science by Ted Corcoran, former international president of Toastmasters and now a leadership coach:

Five points to develop your sales pitch presentation

- **Get attention.** Set up an introduction to your presentation that will generate immediate attention and interest. This may involve using a story, an illustrative example, a video clip or simply a question or a statistic.

- **Brief overview.** Give your audience a brief overview of what you will talk about.

- **Main points.** Provide between three and five salient points, with examples for your argument or your case. Here is the opportunity to provide client testimonials, sample work and demonstrations of how what you offer can meet your client's needs.

- **Summary.** Summarise your main points, with distinct reference to how each one meets your prospective client's requirement.

- **Motivational ending.** Outline the purpose for your speech, whether you want prospective clients to be informed for discussion purposes, to consider your proposal or to choose you over other suppliers.

Source: Ted Corcoran

Sales follow-up

The best tool to use for sales follow-up is your diary. Even if the result of your sales pitch or tender document is negative, keep the lines of communication open with the prospective client so that you can avail of future opportunities.

Promotion:
Five media you can afford to pay for

13

'Half the money I spend on advertising is wasted. The trouble is, I don't know which half.'

John Wanamaker, US department store merchant (1838–1922)

How do you want the person you are addressing to feel, think or act following your communication? The best communications are designed to elicit a response from the receiver.[65] There are many ways to communicate, but some are expensive and not necessarily appropriate when it comes to attracting people to a professional practice. I have found that the best communications methods are less expensive and more personal, and can be executed more thoughtfully.

The first thing you need to consider in any promotional initiative is the message you want to convey to the audience. Are you simply letting people know that you exist and generating awareness for your brand? Or are you going a step further by enticing people to try a particular service? Are you offering a special deal to attract clients?

When your existing clients, or prospective new clients, are looking for someone to advise them, you want your professional practice to be the first one that they think of. Marketing promotions can help to keep you at the forefront of people's minds.

I have mentioned the importance of having an **integrated communications strategy**. This simply means that you thread a common message, language and approach through all your communications.

Your message will have both content and format. Preparing the content calls for you to understand your target audience and what will motivate members of this audience to respond. In turn, the format of what you say should arouse interest and, hopefully, positive action.[66] Make sure that your message is clear and easily understood, and that it makes sense to the people you are addressing. This means giving clear and

---

65. Kotler, Hayes and Bloom, *Marketing Professional Services* (Prentice Hall Press, 2002)
66. Kotler, Hayes and Bloom, *Marketing Professional Services* (as above)

Client Science – The Five Cs Marketing Plan for Professionals

accessible contact details, easy-to-complete forms or registration processes when they sign up with you, useful and informative updates to help them get maximum benefit from what you offer, and relevant and factual information to guide them even when they are not transacting with you.

A useful guide that I recommend to help you with both the content and format of marketing communications is *This Business of Writing* by Terry Prone and Kieran Lyons.[67]

Choose your communications vehicle

Your next step is to choose the media through which you will communicate your message. The vehicles that you select should be driven by your clients, what media they favour, and what information you need to provide in order to attract a response from them.

Here are five cost-effective methods of communication for professionals in practice:

Figure 27. Five media you can afford to pay for

Promotion –
Five media you can afford to pay for

Direct-response marketing

Newsletters and testimonals

Sponsorship

Conferences and seminars

Advertising

---

67. Terry Prone and Kieran Lyons, *This Business of Writing* (Chartered Accountants Ireland, 2006)

Once you have chosen your communications methods, put a plan in place. Set priorities and timelines for each item of the plan. Always seek feedback from clients and employees on new ideas so that you can make improvements as you go along.

1. Direct-response marketing

Direct marketing can be described as communications that are carefully targeted at individual clients to obtain an immediate response. The tools used include mail, telephone, email and some types of advertising.

As you meet key influencers, collaborators and potential clients, there is one question that you should ask every one of them: **'Can I add your name to our mailing list?'**

This simple question is one of the most powerful marketing tools there is. Obtaining a person's permission to connect with them at a later date is invaluable – and, if networking is your thing, you will soon find that you have built up a substantial database of people who are happy for you to communicate with them.

There is the right way to do direct marketing and the wrong way. As a professional, you need to be careful about how you approach sending mail to potential clients. For a start, make sure that people you send unsolicited mail to are not on the National Directory Database, which allows people to voluntarily opt out of receiving unsolicited direct marketing in the form of mail, phone calls and emails.

Occasionally, if you have a compelling, unusual and suitably appealing new service to offer, and you want to inform a group of people in your target market simultaneously, then direct mail may achieve that goal for you.

Whatever the nature of your direct mail piece, be it an invitation to a seminar or a letter asking the recipient to consider your services, make sure it includes an obvious way to respond. The **call to action**, as it is referred to, is the critical part of the art of direct mail.

Decide what action you want the person who receives your correspondence to take. This is the wrong forum for educating prospective clients. Your aim is to whet their appetite; then, hopefully, they will either be ready to accept your follow-up call, or will call or email you.

There are **advantages to direct mail**:

- It is cost-effective, particularly when appealing to a personal audience.
- It is can be creative and well-received, if done well.
- It can be personalised.

On the other hand, there is so much direct mail arriving in post boxes on a daily basis that it is hard to get someone to read unsolicited mail, let alone respond to it. Look at your own mailbox. Consider what works for you personally and what turns you off. Direct mail that isn't well thought-out can achieve such a limited response that the money spent on it is wasted. (The standard response rate for direct mail is 5 percent or less.)

When putting together a direct mail piece, be sure that it:

- creates the right impression in the mind of the person you are writing to;

- provides a solution that the person will find compelling – in other words, make sure it is presented in a way that makes the recipient curious to find out more;

- includes a way for the person who receives it to respond.

Make sure your email or postal address mailing list is accurate. No one wants to receive a letter with their name spelt incorrectly – or addressed to a dead person, a retired employee or a person who moved to another company years ago. This is no way to build trust, and it could be the last connection you will have with that particular target name.

Carefully evaluate the number and kind of responses you receive after the direct mail campaign so that you can determine its effectiveness. This will also serve as a way for you to improve your future direct mail efforts.

An important, and often underrated, aspect of direct response marketing is your correspondence with your existing clients. Think of every piece of correspondence with a client to be a valuable opportunity to communicate your values, your practice and the importance of the relationship with the client.

It is therefore important to avoid being overly officious and to inject personality where possible into client communications. Some documents, particularly legal or medical, have to adhere to a strict code of language. However, it is important not to overlook the fact that the recipient of your communications is always an individual. Aim to accompany your formal communication with a less formal note, or a preceding phone call where possible to maintain a more personal touch. If you rely solely on formal correspondence to interact with a client, they may consider you to be remote or inaccessible. This could have an impact on their decision to transact with you at a later date.

Why should you expect a formal letter back in response to your correspondence? Think about customer convenience and take the approach that this accountant took to his correspondence:

'Where we are writing to a client requesting a specific response to questions, we don't expect them to have to write a letter back to us with all the details. We know that that is wasting the client's time. Instead, we leave a wide margin of space on the letter, so that the client can write in their answers rather than having to go to the trouble of typing a new letter. Most of the time, that is all that is needed.'   **Accountant**

Business card

An Irish accountant, Eamonn Leahy won an international award for the best business card. His card was profiled in the book, *It's in the Cards.*[68] Your business card is one of the most vital direct response mechanisms that you can give to anyone. Usually, it has your brand name, logo and contact details relating exclusively to you, as well as a brief reflection of your type of business and your values.

Think about how to differentiate your business with a message that reflects your value proposition. There is ample space on the back of the business card for details of the services you can offer clients, so take advantage of that opportunity, and make sure that any prospective client that gets your card is clear about what you can do for them.

LEAHY & CO

Clients Recommend us

CHARTERED ACCOUNTANTS

EAMONN LEAHY

PARTNER

Tel D3 : (01) 853 7000
Tel D14: (01) 492 7012

---

68. Ivan R. Misner, Candice Bailly, Dan Georgevich, *It's in the Cards* (Paradigm Publishing, 2003)

Invoices

Another piece of correspondence that requires a direct response from clients is the invoice. Invoices could be described as the 'cold face' of your practice, but why should they be? They are an important part of the negotiated agreement between you and your client. Without payment, your client is not a client, but a charity case. Invoices should be anything but cold.

Make your invoices clear and easy to respond to:

* Send the invoice to the person who can authorise and send the invoice for processing. Too many invoices go astray because they are not properly addressed.

* Include clear details of your business, including a contact number for queries and easy-to-follow payment instructions.

* Provide transparent, accurate and well-documented details about what you are invoicing for.

Applied Science

* Always include a note, preferably handwritten, saying: 'Thank you for the business.'

One accountant that I interviewed communicates with every one of his clients twelve times per year. He begins the year with a satisfaction survey (discussed in **Chapter 7**) to find out if his clients are happy with the service he is providing and whether they have suggestions for other services or ways to deliver that could help him to improve. Secondly, he feeds back the results to his clients by email, saying: 'Thank you to those who completed my survey; here are the specific improvements that I intend to make as a result of your feedback.'

Three times per year, he writes to clients, sometimes with a letter, sometimes with an information leaflet or a copy of an article, whitepaper, or newspaper cutting containing information on a topic directly related to a client's particular business. It might be a change in tax legislation, or information about a grant, or data relating to the sector in which the client operates.

His sixth piece of communication is his annual budget briefing, summarised in a simple but nicely branded booklet. The seventh, eighth and ninth pieces of communication are the newsletter, which he sends out three times each year.

He sends out a reminder of when his clients' annual returns are due, together with notice of on offer whereby, if they submit all their tax-related information by a certain date, he will provide a discount. That is communication number ten.

Communication number eleven is a letter asking for referrals from his clients.

Number twelve is a Christmas card with a voucher for money off any new services his clients may avail of in the new year.

2. Collateral: brochures, newsletters and client testimonials

All twelve pieces of marketing communication sent by the accountant in our example are directly relevant to his clients. The material is sent to each person as a thoughtful gift rather than as a hard sell. All of your marketing material – or 'collateral' as it is often referred to – should adopt this client-orientated approach.

Many of you will find a brochure useful to help you describe the services you offer. The types of brochures you need very much depend on the type of practice you run. A brochure is very useful when it describes your practice, your values, and the products and services you offer to clients in a way that helps them understand how you can solve their problem or satisfy their particular need. This means that brochures should not contain lists of products, features or benefits; they should adopt a problem-and-solution approach.

Applied Science

The brochure should be written in the client's language – which is usually not technical language. This is broadly how a brochure should be arranged:

- **Your company perspective.** Set out the credentials of your practice as it relates to the needs of your client.

- **Your client's perspective**. Include details of the product or service as they are applied to your client's needs and expectations. A suitable format is as follows:

  - Set out a typical customer need or problem.

  - Show how your particular product or service is designed to solve that need or problem.

  - Demonstrate how the product or service has worked for another client to solve or meet the particular problem.

  - Give an illustration: an example of how the product or service is applied in a particular scenario is useful.

- **Contact details.** Contact name, position, business address, email, contact number plus an alternative person, so that there is always a backup contact.

Client testimonial

If you really want to prove how good you are, get someone else to talk for you. There is great merit in producing a client testimonial:

- The client gets some profile.

- You get to put out an information piece that actively shows how you solved a client's need or problem.

- The most valuable aspect of the client testimonial is that it demonstrates to other potential clients, who have similar requirements, how you can solve their needs. This is one of the most powerful forms of communication.

Newsletters

Newsletters, if done well, are an opportunity to celebrate business success and achievement between you, your clients, your co-workers and those you collaborate with. Client case studies, if approved by the client for publicity, make excellent content for newsletters.

Newsletters are also useful for highlighting new service updates, and profiles of your employees. You can provide details of upcoming or recently hosted events, seminars and conferences. They also provide a forum to show how your expertise can help clients adapt to a new legislative, economic or market environment. A newsletter can also help to highlight your commitment to corporate social responsibility. As much as possible, focus on clients and how they benefit from your services.

Newsletters should not be used as a sales pitch, a brochure or an advertisement. This type of newsletter is seldom read unless it contains highly relevant special deals. A newsletter should be informative, useful and relevant to a client. Overbearing and incorrect statements should not be used because they will create a negative perception of your practice in the mind of the client.

Increasingly, newsletters are distributed by email instead of as a printed copy. There are a number of web-based packages such as Newsweaver that can help you create a highly professional publication. After initial set-up costs, an emailed newsletter tends to be cheaper and more flexible than print in the long run.

3. Sponsorships

I began my career in AIB Bank's sponsorship division. We sponsored a large number of events both locally and nationally. We were big sponsors of local sporting fixtures such as GAA, soccer and golf events. We sponsored school activities: debating, business start-up competitions, and even a campaign for crossing the road safely. At national level, we ran a new business start-up competition with *The Gay Byrne Hour*, the Better Ireland Awards and agri-tourism awards. I learned that sponsorship is highly effective because you can secure great publicity while giving back to the community.

Sponsorship does not have to take the form of an expensive national campaign. Sometimes putting money into a golf event and entertaining your golf-loving clients can pay dividends. Getting to spend hours of quality time with important clients is a sensible investment. Similarly, an investment in a cause-related event can motivate young talent in your practice, or customers who are passionate about a particular cause.

You can reap great benefits from good sponsorship – the important thing is to work hard to get publicity for it. A sponsorship is a formal contract between your practice and an external organisation in relation to one or more events – you gain publicity rights and brand benefits in return for sponsorship money.

If you choose to sponsor a local football tournament, for example, what are the benefits that you might expect to receive from the organisers? Here are five benefits that you should expect to receive in return for sponsorship money:

Joint publicity. A launch photograph to announce the sponsorship, and details of it sent to the press and to the local community.

Sponsorship acknowledgement. The organisers would thank you as sponsor for your involvement when they are advertising and sending out publicity statements about the sponsorship.

Logo and advertisement. To have your logo and information about your practice, or an advertisement, in a tournament information guide, as signage at the playing grounds and on all promotional material.

Speaking opportunity. One of your team gets the opportunity to speak at a pre-tournament or post-tournament event – lunch, dinner or drinks party.

Presentation to winners. A member of your practice would present the prize to the winning team and be photographed for the media release announcing the winner.

The cost of sponsorship events varies considerably. Choose organisations whose values fit with those of your practice, and look for natural linkages. Preferably, you want to sponsor events that offer you the opportunity to get your name, logo and team in front of existing and prospective clients.

One of the most successful international sponsorships by a professional services firm is the Ernst & Young Entrepreneur of the Year Awards. Nominees from over 135 countries compete for the 'Entrepreneur of the Year' title in their respective region. Then the top tier of winners come together to compete for the world prize each year. Short-listed competitors are given a range of opportunities, including team-building challenges, executive education and a CEO retreat. The benefit for Ernst & Young is that their team get to associate and build relationships with the top entrepreneurs in each country. Through live TV presentations of their awards ceremonies, they have the added benefit of publicising their dedication to entrepreneurship to a wider business audience.

Sponsorships like this one positively reflect the brand values of the sponsoring organisation. There is a high investment cost for Ernst & Young in their global sponsorship, but smaller practices can take on more affordable sponsorships locally. The success of a good sponsorship depends in part on how creative the organisers are.

Science Fact Some organisations avoid sponsoring individuals and sponsor teams instead. Teams offer greater security and lower risk, as this announcement by Accenture in 2009 illustrates:

Accenture becomes first sponsor to drop Tiger Woods completely

Global consulting firm says it 'determined that he is no longer the right representative for its advertising' after his decision to take a break from golf after admitting to infidelity. ...Accenture released a statement saying it was ending its business agreement with Woods, who had represented the company for six years.

Source: Los Angeles Times, 14 December 2009

4. Conferences and seminars

The key to a brilliant conference or seminar is the topic chosen. If you choose a topic that is highly relevant to your target audience – an area that they want or need to know about – then you will achieve great success.

When making any kind of presentation, be as dynamic as possible and make yourself available after the presentation to answer questions individually. Leaving immediately after making a speech will lead to missed opportunities for making new client contacts.

I find that instead of providing handouts on the day, it is better to go back to attendees later by email with a weblink to the presentations. Writing to participants after the seminar also gives you another opportunity to interact with your audience. It is a chance to ask for feedback – 'Did our seminar meet your needs?' or 'Have you suggestions for other seminar topics?' – as well as a way to make direct contact and to provide your contact details.

Applied Science

> 'Conferences and seminars are the best for us. When one of our legal partners is invited to speak at an event, we generally find that we will attract enquiries from potential clients, nearly every time.'
>
> **Lawyer**

5. Advertising

Advertising does not have to be expensive in order to be effective. If your target market is a particular business sector, consider the industry trade publications that relate to that audience. These publications tend to be less expensive than national print media. Apart from the usual newspaper and magazine slots, advertisements can be inserted into conference brochures, sports and theatre programmes, and even school and college event programmes at relatively low cost.

Here are five things to keep in mind when designing an advertisement:

Consider your target audience. Your priority is to ensure that your advertising reaches your target audience. Brief your marketing consultant or advertising agency clearly on whom exactly you want to target. The discussion in Part II about your value proposition, target audience and market niches is particularly relevant for helping you and your advertising executive produce an advert that will attract attention from the right individuals.

Limit the amount of text. People don't read advertisements line by line; most prefer to skim them quickly. Keep your message simple and up-front. In your advertisement include a maximum of three key messages that you want people to remember. Highlight those messages in order of priority. Include your strapline and a reference to how you provide value for money – your value proposition.

Aim for 'cut-through'. There is so much advertising in the marketplace that most of it goes unnoticed. To avoid that problem, spend time looking at advertisements that engage your attention. Work with your agency to find a layout and colour scheme that is striking and distinctive, and that reflects the brand that you have worked hard to build.

Choose suitable images. Make sure that your imagery and text reproduces well in print. Images can often look fantastic in high resolution but may print badly in newspapers – and this is a poor use of your budget. Carefully select the image to reflect your particular brand.

Have a stock advertisement pre-prepared. Don't wait until you are asked to provide an advertisement; get an advertisement made up and have it ready to go. This means that you can take advantage of opportunities that come up to place an advert at low cost. Make sure that you have an advert designed that can be reproduced in both landscape and portrait versions. Depending on your marketing budget, you will also need a variety of advert sizes.

Here are five suitable places to advertise for clients:

Science Fact

Newspapers

According to the *Media Directory*, print advertising – in national and regional press, and in magazines – remains the most popular advertising medium, accounting for two-thirds of advertising spending. Local newspapers are particularly powerful and cost-effective in Ireland. Use them both for advertising and to build profile for your practice in the locality.

Magazines

Magazines are effective when it comes to targeting particular sectors of the market, but I seldom advertise without combining editorial as well. I prefer to supply an article on a topical aspect of the business that I am advertising to accompany the advertisement. I always ask for an opportunity to produce an article; this can be placed either in the same issue as the advertisement, or a subsequent issue. As you might imagine, editorial has a higher readership than advertising.

Radio

For large practices, local radio can be a remarkably cost-effective and powerful form of advertising. The cost is generally not in the production of a radio advertisement, but in its placement. National radio stations are more expensive and will achieve strong profile for national brands. Local radio stations can present good opportunities for a medium-sized practice to generate brand awareness. You might also consider sponsoring a particular programme on local radio. Again, this can be done at relatively low cost.

Online

Online advertising represents about 7 percent of the total advertising spend in Ireland at present, but it is much higher abroad. The trend is moving towards online advertising: it is less expensive to design and place, and the results can be tracked far more easily. If there is a trend among your clients, or potential clients, towards particular websites, you might want to consider placing an advertisement there. This type of advertising is good for brand awareness and to drive traffic to your website. The drawback for online advertising is that you cannot guarantee either the quantity or the quality of clients recruited via the Web.

Directories

There are mixed views about how valuable directories are for information about practices. Some directories are extremely useful, like the *Bankers Almanac* for international banking payment details, or international legal directories containing names of firms that specialise in particular aspects of law. Other people claim that directories do not tend to yield the best type of clients, and most professionals prefer to get introductions from people who are familiar with their practices.

My advice is to have a presence in every directory that is relevant to your target audience. Clients tend to use online directories nowadays: ensure that any directory insert you submit online is not only print-friendly but also presents a superior image of your practice when it is placed alongside those of competitors.

Be aware of advertising guidelines

As a professional, it is incumbent on you to use advertisements which are of a high standard. The Law Society's advertising regulations for solicitors are a useful guide for any professional practice. They advise people to avoid placing advertisements for your practice that[69]:

- are likely to bring the profession into disrepute

- are in bad taste

- reflect unfavourably on other solicitors

- assert that a solicitor has specialist knowledge superior to other solicitors

- are false or misleading

- are contrary to public policy.

It is also important to refer to the Consumer Protection Code.

A note on foreign language translation

In today's multi-ethnic society, advertisements, application forms, websites and other marketing material are increasingly displayed in a number of languages. This is a tremendously clever way of attracting a wider client base. Try to find a translator who can do justice to your carefully thought-out, client-friendly information. There are several highly reputable agencies that specialise in translating marketing information.

Always arrange for a trusted source to double-check translated work to be certain that the meaning of what you intend putting out is clear and accurate.

---

69. Extract from the Law Society of Ireland website, www.lawsociety.ie

Public Relations:
Five ways to get free publicity

14

'Publicity is the life of this culture — insofar as without publicity, capitalism could not survive — and at the same time publicity is its dream.'

John Berger, *Ways of Seeing*

One of the great marketing experts, Philip Kotler, a professor at Harvard Business School, describes PR as 'building good relations with the company's various publics by obtaining favourable publicity, building up a good "corporate image" and handling or heading off unfavourable rumours, stories and events'.

There are a number of elements in Professor Kotler's definition that are relevant for a professional practice. The first relates to taking a proactive approach to building relationships with the community and the public. In Part II, I showed how the local community takes a view of your practice with regard to local interaction, your premises, and your overall reputation. You can influence your target audience if you use public relations. It is possible to communicate a positive message by using the various publications, both print and online, that your target audience is likely to read. This part of public relations is not particularly difficult; in fact, you probably have the material and the tools already.

The second element is about building up the image of your practice – what Kotler refers to as your 'corporate image'. There are a number of very subtle ways of building an image. Image building can be as simple as being photographed at an event or as sophisticated as staging a launch to announce a ground-breaking new service for clients.

The third element that Kotler refers to is handling unfavourable rumours, stories and events. This is the reputation management aspect of PR. You only need to read the newspapers to observe how reputations can be made or lost thanks to a single newspaper article. Depending on the size of your practice, you may have a PR team, or you may have access to the services of a PR agency. Reputation management PR is a particularly specialised skill. It requires careful thought and preparation, and I would advise getting expert advice on media handling, particularly if you are faced with potentially unfavourable publicity.

At the same time, you can manage a great deal of your own PR and generate good quality publicity for a low cost.

How to write a press release

Observe the style of the publication you are writing for. An article is much more likely to be taken up if the style in which it is written matches the style and tone of the magazine or newspaper. Check out other similar articles that the publication has run lately, and ensure that your article conforms to this style.

Here are the salient points when it comes to writing a press release. A press release should be structured like a news story because it will occupy the same sort of space as any other news story. Observe how news stories are structured in your newspaper. The most important detail of the story is usually found in the first two paragraphs. Therefore, the press release should aim to answer these key questions – Who? What? When? Where? Why? How? – in those opening paragraphs.[70]

Your press release should[71]:

- Have a short, vivid, attention-grabbing headline. Again, think of the language of your readers, rather than your own more technical formulation.

- Feature answers to the key questions in the first couple of paragraphs. This means that if you only get enough space for the first paragraph, at least your main points will appear.

- Use active as opposed to passive language. For example, 'Dog bites man' rather than 'Man is bitten by dog'.

- Contain mainly short sentences. Break up your text into chunks that your readers can digest easily.

- Be relevant. It must contain topical information, relevant and of interest to the readers of the publication from which you are seeking publicity.

---

70. Terry Prone, Kieran Lyons, *This Business of Writing* (Chartered Accountants Ireland, 2006)
71. Terry Prone, Kieran Lyons, *This Business of Writing* (see above)

Most press releases are submitted via email. The layout for a press release should be as follows:

How to lay out a press release

State release date. Either 'For immediate release' or 'Embargo – 30 April 2011'

The headline. This must be meaningful and relevant.

The introductory paragraphs: What, When, Why, Who, Where, How

Seventy-five percent of professionals have never used public relations to generate profile. The incredible thing is that they have so much of value to offer people: new information, advice and future predictions. Give us a strong introduction. Tell us something we don't already know. Make it newsworthy, topical and relevant to the times and the people.

If your introductory paragraph is sufficiently interesting, a journalist will want to know more. Now include a quote from your lead spokesperson. Be more detailed about your idea, advice or prediction, and keep us hooked. Who are the main players? Where, when, how and why did all this come about? What can we do about it?

Your end paragraphs. Try to sell everything that's interesting about it. Why is this issue important? Why should people pay attention to your campaign? What do you hope to achieve? How can people help? Don't make it too long, and keep it easy to read.

Don't go on and on. Include the crucial information, any relevant statistics, and important details like dates and places. By now, the journalist will be getting bored, so let them know you are available to give more information or even an interview, and finish off with[72]:

[Ends]

For further information:
Name
Title
Tel
Email
Website address

If you have supporting images, tell them about these at the end.

---

72. Adapted from youthnation.com

A sample press release

This press release, issued by the Seapoint Dental Clinic in Dublin, illustrates how a professional in practice can attract publicity using observations from their everyday work that appeal to the wider audience.

Daily grind is leading to more dental checks

Grinding and clenching teeth, which is increasingly common and exacerbated by stress, is leading to a high number of people attending dentists with cracked teeth, according to Dr Thomas Linehan of the Seapoint Clinic in Blackrock, Dublin.

"Many people are completely unaware that they grind their teeth, as they often do it only when they are asleep. They only become aware of the problem when they have discomfort or pain, or notice small lines or cracks on the teeth", says Dr Linehan.

While the tough economic times are an obvious factor in higher stress levels, Dr Linehan also points out that people who chew ice, bite their fingernails, or habitually chew on pens are also placing their teeth at risk. "Symptoms of a tooth crack include sensitivity to temperature change, both hot and cold, the separating or loosening of small parts of a tooth, and pain when biting down.

The good news is that a range of treatments is available, including bonding, crowns, veneers, or even implants for badly damaged teeth."

Ends

Source: The Metro/Herald (3 February 2010)

Who do you send your press release to?

When you are ready to distribute the press release, you will need to contact local journalists or the editor of the publication that you want to send your press release to. Find out how they prefer to receive the press release – whether by email, fax or on a memory key.

For more comprehensive guidelines on writing and producing press releases, I recommend the book *This Business of Writing* by Terry Prone and Kieran Lyons, which provides detailed guidelines, as well as the do's and don'ts of how to craft a press release.

Here are five ways to attract positive publicity:

Figure 28. Public relations: Five ways to attract free publicity

Public Relations
Five ways to attract free publicity

1. Help a journalist

2. Supply topical stories

3. Write for industry journals

4. Hold a press launch

5. Publicise awards

1. Help a journalist

Journalists are always interested in – and indeed in need of – good quality news stories. Your first consideration in producing any press release is to consider your target audience. (Who will this press release appeal to?) Then build alliances with local journalists or those linked to the publications that address the people you want to talk to. For example, a journalist may be asked to cover the green energy sector. A lawyer targeting clients who operate in this area could provide interesting stories, explanations and quotes to journalists to give them a different angle on the sector.

You can make a journalist's job a lot easier by providing information relating not only to the services you provide but also to the issues you come across, and can resolve for the publication's readers. Target specific journalists who would value the type of information and analysis that you can provide. In other words, help journalists achieve their own goals. The benefit to you, over time, are references to you and your business in articles written by these journalists.

If the nature of your practice shows high potential for media coverage, you could put together a press pack and send it to the journalists that cover your particular sector and target market. A press pack typically contains the following information:

- Practice credentials: length of time in business, size, employee numbers and location

- Details of the solutions that you provide for clients as they relate specifically to the journalist's target audience

- Areas of expertise and topics that you or members of your team could competently comment on

- Calendar of events: dates for related market surveys that you produce, as well as conferences, seminars and other opportunities that will give the journalist information to work with

- Contact details for the designated media spokesperson or team members, including out-of-hours mobile numbers

2. Supply topical and engaging stories

Journalists rarely write stories from unsolicited marketing press releases. By marketing press releases, I mean ones that try to sell a product or service to the public. Journalists see these type of stories for what they are: advertising, or advertorial. Keep in mind that newspaper editors get hundreds of stories faxed, mailed and emailed to them every day. Only a fraction of these press releases get published.

So, how can you make stories from your practice newsworthy? The stories or articles that are published are always highly topical and very relevant to the readership of the publication. The best way to fit your story into a publication is to study back issues and discover what type of article fits, how it is written, what the tone of the article is, and how it is pitched. Are articles 'highbrow' and sophisticated, with technical language tailored to a target audience in a particular field of expertise, or are they produced in a more simplified language to appeal to a broader range of readers?

One way to have your story picked up by the press is to take an angle that is particularly topical or amusing. Here is a particularly attention-grabbing (Christmas) PR release by a doctor in Australia:

Santa should get off his sleigh and walk

Santa should share Rudolf's snack of carrots and celery sticks rather than brandy and mince pies and swap his reindeer for a bike or a walk, says a public health expert in the Christmas issue published on www.bmj.com today.

Dr Nathan Grills, from Monash University in Australia, says the current image of Santa promotes obesity, drink-driving, speeding and a generally unhealthy lifestyle. He argues that 'Santa only needs to affect health by 0.1 percent to damage millions of lives' and that it would be better if his popularity was used to promote healthy living.

Source: British Medical Journal

The article about Santa works on a number of levels. It is amusing and engaging, but it also has a serious underlying message. It demonstrates the concern felt by Dr Grills about obesity and, as a result, the article profiles this doctor positively among his target audience.

If you are involved in a cutting-edge area, from which interesting news stories emanate regularly, then send out regular press releases. Barack Obama's PR machine sends out media releases very regularly to keep the public up to date on progress. You can do the same without too much difficulty. First, produce a stock of varied, topical and interesting stories. Then establish contact with journalists in publications that are looking for newsworthy stories. *The Writers' and Artists' Yearbook*, produced annually, contains details of newspapers, journals and magazines that are open to receiving articles for publication.

3. Write for industry journals

Industry journals are very useful for targeting particular groups of clients. So whether your particular sector is parenting, start-up-businesses, house buyers or the top 1,000 companies, there are journals dedicated to it.

A number of periodicals will publish articles by experts in areas that their readers are particularly interested in for free. Articles that you submit should focus purely on expert thought leadership, rather than advertising your business. However, you get the benefit of having your name, business or practice name and contact details at the bottom of the article for further information.

'We did some analysis of our customer base and we identified sectors that we particularly wanted to target. Three industries stood out for us as excellent in terms of client relationships, profitability and our own expertise. One of these was the tyre trade. We already had a good relationship with the Irish Tyre Industry Association, the organisation that represents manufacturers, importers, wholesalers, retailers, recyclers and equipment for the tyre trade in Ireland. We decided to provide a series of useful and relevant articles for members of the tyre industry about cashflow, invoice financing, investing and foreign exchange in the *Irish Tyre Trade Journal*. The articles were practical in nature, with no sales talk. Our objective was to inform and to provide valuable information to members. In return, we got to profile our brand in that particular sector, and each article had contact details for a team leader at the end, so that anyone interested in learning more could contact us directly.'

Commercial finance director

Once again, *The Writers' and Artists' Yearbook* provides useful contact details for trade and industry publications.

To create newsworthy stories, you could link in with a trade association or representative body to conduct an industry study or survey. Information gathered from polls and surveys lends weight to an article or press release. If the topic is relevant to the public at a particular time, it has a greater chance of being covered by a journalist – provided it is backed by solid, quantitative information.

4. Hold a press launch

If you decide to launch a new service, or a new way of doing things, onto the market, one way to get the message out is to hold a press launch. Invite journalists to a reception, and provide a public relations pack containing a press release detailing the new service, client testimonials and key contact details for further information.

These days, journalists are covering more areas and have fewer resources. Don't expect a big turnout of journalists for your reception, unless you have a really exciting new development to announce. Send a press pack to journalists that can't be there, together with contact details, so they can call if they need further information.

5. Publicise awards

There are two ways for a professional practice to get publicity for an award. The first is to sponsor or present the award, and the second is to win the award.

Awards are a great way to reward success. Over the past decade, award schemes have sprung up in almost every industry. Look at which awards schemes are applicable to your target audience, and discover whether you can sponsor one of the awards. I mentioned the Ernst & Young Entrepreneur of the Year awards in the last chapter, and how partners of Ernst & Young in each of the countries got the opportunity to build relationships with the relevant finalists. Sponsoring awards gives you the chance to make contact with shortlisted nominees and to interact with them. In addition, you get the chance to be photographed presenting the award, for publicity purposes.

Entering for and winning an award is a great way of letting your clients and potential clients know how you perform against your peers. There is a benefit in being shortlisted for an award, even if you do not win. It takes time and resources to submit an application for an award, but the media coverage may be worth it.

The great benefits of awards are that they generate press coverage that you don't have to organise yourself. Awards help you stand out from your competitors, and they give reassurance to your clients. They also give you credibility within your sector, and they can be useful in recruiting and retaining staff.[73]

---

73. Annmarie Hanlon, *QuickWin Marketing: Answers to Your Top 100 Marketing Questions* (Oak Tree Press, 2009)

Digital Media:
Five ways to engage clients

15

'*Social media is the collection of tools and online spaces available to help individuals and businesses to accelerate their information and communication needs.*'

Axel Schultze

The highly successful Irish TV journalist Mark Little recently took a leave of absence from television presenting to pursue a project combining digital media and global journalism. Little said:

'The rise of social media platforms like YouTube, Twitter and Facebook provide an opportunity for journalists to change the way we report the world. I would like to take a more direct role in that transformation.'

Mark Little is not the first to find digital media compelling. Most major global companies now tune in to social media to obtain information on what their customers and their employees are saying about them and to monitor trends and competitor initiatives, and to find new ideas. Some would say that the future is happening online.

On President Barack Obama's website, there is a section called 'Obama Everywhere'; it shows the Internet locations where the president has established a specific Web presence. He has a presence on most of the mainstream networking sites, including: LinkedIn, Twitter, Facebook, BlackPlanet, MySpace, YouTube and Flickr.

There was a time when we had to rely on journalists and reporters to filter news, images and stories through print, wireless and television channels, before we were able to find out what was going on in the world. Digital media has changed all that.

Digital media is different from traditional media because the power of information-sharing is in the hands of the people. When protesters in Iran wanted to transmit terrible scenes of violence to the rest of the world, they could do so via the micro-blog Twitter, and their stories were spread globally. Digital media is immensely powerful, and we all have to take notice of it.

Suddenly, the hierarchical nature of information flow has changed. Now, the news we receive is not necessarily filtered through journalists and other influencers, who put their own spin on it. Right now, the power of information is with the people.

Digital media relates to the Internet, e-commerce, mobile phone technology, social networking sites (such as LinkedIn and Facebook), blogs, microblogs (such as Twitter) and image and video domains (such as Flickr and YouTube). Not all of these digital media are relevant to a professional in practice; some, such as Bebo and Facebook are more suitable for social interaction. I have here chosen five areas of digital media that you should be aware of, and indeed should participate in. None of them are difficult to implement, and all are useful in helping you to profile who you are personally and what your professional practice is about.

Why is digital media important to your practice?

The compelling reason why none of us can ignore digital media is that clients use it every day. They use it to compare your service and image to that of other providers. They use it to locate your office, access your phone number and find your competitors. They use it to place orders, book appointments and find out how satisfied clients are with services provided by various companies before they purchase.

Krishna De, a leading expert on digital and social media, argues that professionals should be aware of the power of the Internet for business.[74] Ninety-three percent of European business people now have access to the Internet, and e-commerce accounts for 12 percent of EU business.[75]

That means that most of the business clients of professional firms are online regularly and using the Web to gather information about service providers. However, you don't have to do a hard sell on the Web. It is not all about having a shopping cart on your Internet site. A good presence is required so that people can find out who you are. The Web is now part of the customer journey that was discussed in **Chapter 10**.

---

74. Adapted from an article by Krishna De on www.krishnade.com

75. Source: Shaun Nicholls, 'E-commerce accounts for 12 percent of EU business', www.computing.co.uk, 10 January 2010

An old dog learns e-tricks

Jack Welch, former CEO of GE, speaks candidly for a large number of professionals who feel they can't possibly use digital media. In a speech in 1999, he told an audience:

> 'E-business is the biggest game in town, probably the biggest idea that has come along in a hundred years, and let's be honest, we could have missed it. My age and my experience were against me on this one. I thought it was nonsense at first. It was Jane, my wife, who finally got me into e-commerce. I saw her doing all kinds of stuff online: Jane basically lives at E*Trade. Or we'd be going somewhere on vacation and she'd show me a virtual tour. So I got started. I'm totally hooked.'[76]

What are the main forms of digital media that professionals can use? Here is a brief synopsis of the most prominent and most talked about digital media at present:

Figure 29. Digital Media: Five ways to hook clients

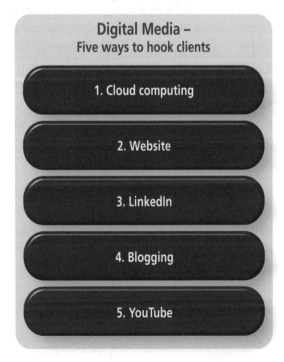

Digital Media –
Five ways to hook clients

1. Cloud computing
2. Website
3. LinkedIn
4. Blogging
5. YouTube

---

76. Noel M. Tichy and Stratford Sherman, 'Control Your Destiny or Someone Else Will' (Collins, 2005)

1. Cloud computing

IT is used extensively by practices of all types to manage and control operations, to improve productivity and to help service clients. Importantly, you do not have to own or manage IT in order to use it. 'Cloud computing' allows you to download the software you need from the Internet and to access applications anytime and anywhere, once you have online access.

Google is the best-known form of cloud computing. However, most people use cloud computing also for email, Internet banking and booking flights online. Cloud computing allows a large group of subscribers to access services that would cost a lot more to avail of if they were specifically customised to the needs of one business, practice or individual. The other benefit is that cloud computing tends to be a pay-as-you-go service, or an operating expense, instead of the traditional capital expenditure that practices had to pay out for software and services within the office. No software licences are required, no services or communications infrastructure is needed, and there are no backups to carry out, because everything is stored 'in the cloud'.

Cloud computing applications can be as simple as having an appointment-booking service online or as sophisticated as conducting a major transaction online, with you and the client working on the same documents simultaneously. Cloud computing has many benefits. The first overarching advantage is that a huge proportion of clients now want to transact online. As we have seen, 93 percent of business people use the Internet on a regular basis. Using the Internet can significantly improve service to clients and can speed up turnaround.

Your clients are now using technology such as iPhones and Blackberrys to keep in touch. Cloud computing facilitates this in a way that ordinary correspondence or software packages never could. It also helps to satisfy the green energy agenda and the desire for the paperless office.

 One of the most interesting interactive sites I have come across is smallbusinessscan.com. It is an ideal site for practitioners seeking to give or receive business advice and support.

Smallbusinesscan.com

A team of three entrepreneurs: Ron Immink, Greg Byrne and Fionan Murray set up the website smallbusinesscan.com, a platform designed to tap into the collective wisdom of entrepreneurs and give business people a place to ask each other for help and advice, 365/24/7. This website is based on research that shows that entrepreneurs prefer to talk to other entrepreneurs when looking for advice and support.

The site is designed to be run entirely by entrepreneurs *for* entrepreneurs. The platform has three key elements:

- Content that features good news stories of entrepreneurs doing well, advisory articles, podcasts, and videos.

- There is a decision grid structured according to four business growth stages. This open content section provides advice on money, management and marketing appropriate to the individual business. Here entrepreneurs can post their own articles and share experiences. The aim is to become an open source depository of authentic content, for and by entrepreneurs.

- An Insights Xchange where users can share insights, ask other entrepreneurs questions and look for advice, support and introductions to potential customers.

Applied Science   Another example of cloud computing is propertytaxonline.ie, established by Claire O'Connor:

Propertytaxonline.ie

Claire O'Connor, a tax consultant, recognised that a significant number of people (both in Ireland and the UK) had bought investment properties abroad and were required to submit tax returns in Ireland (or UK) and the country where they purchased the property if they were receiving rental income. So she set up www.propertytaxonline.ie.

Claire identified her client's need for a simplified, cost effective and easy solution to filing rental income tax returns on a worldwide basis. The service she devised with business partner Simon Gould is an online tax return service, specialising in (but not limited to) individuals owning a rental property and their obligations to file a tax return in both the location of the relevant investment property and their tax-resident jurisdiction.

The advantage of this service is that it can be accessed anywhere in the world in any chosen language because it is online. It is aimed at clients who do not have the time, knowledge or language fluency to file these tax returns in the appropriate countries.

Propertytaxonline.ie plans to integrate their online system with the software from the Revenue organisations in the various countries they deal with including the Irish Revenue Commissioners' system ROS.

A third example is doctors.net.uk:

Doctors.net.uk

This company was launched in 1998, when the web was barely off the ground. The business needed to build a critical mass of doctors so the networking effect of a working community would create its own momentum. Without a large, active membership, they couldn't expect revenues.

In order to maximise a limited budget and give credibility to a new source of information, education and collaboration for the medical profession, they built partnerships with powerful existing medical institutions as they needed their credibility within the profession. These, in turn, were old institutions, struggling to establish a presence in the new world of the Internet. A joint marketing initiative was set up with the General Medical Council; and the result of a collaborative marketing approach with the Medical Protection Society, the Medical Defence Union and the Medical Sickness Society was membership growth that far exceeded plans, and today www.doctors.net.uk counts virtually every doctor in the UK as a member.

Source: Richard Hall, Brilliant Marketing (Pearson Prentice Hall, 2009)

2. Website

All professionals should have a well-designed website. It is no longer expensive to establish your presence online, though I do advise you to put thought into it. A badly put together website is about as valuable to your brand and reputation as no website at all – and can even have a negative impact on how you are perceived.

The nature and structure of websites has changed dramatically in recent years. If your website just contains a firm profile, brochure details on your services and a list of contacts, then you are out of date. Your website may need to be updated so that you can attract more traffic and provide more relevant information to clients and potential clients about your services. Relevant, interesting, topical content is the way to drive clients to your site.

Top
Scientist

Applied
Science

Krishna De (krishnade.com) provides five elements that are vital to help people find, evaluate and consider you on the Web:

Five ways to get your website noticed

Include contact details

Make sure they are easily accessed on your site, so that people can pick up the phone or email you if they need to.

Photographs

Profile your team. Have photographs of client-facing employees. This creates a personal link before contact is ever made with your firm. A photograph also builds trust; it shows that you are confident about who you and your team are.

Content

Think carefully about the design, usability, and content of your site, and about the words that will be used to search for information in your professional sector. Consider the words your potential clients are likely to use when searching for information in your sphere of influence, and use those words to draw people to your site.[77]

Don't just add brochure-style content to your website. Include articles, white papers, hints and tips, and content that is informative and relevant to your audience. Update it regularly – in fact, very regularly – and be ahead of your peers in terms of content relevance.

Update your website frequently

Keep your website as up-to-date as possible. Many websites have out of date information about the practice profile, services and accolades. Keep your information up-to-date and you are far more likely to attract search engine attention. Continually update your added-value information such as links to new books, and other relevant and topical websites and affiliate organisations.

---

77. Adapted from an article by Krishna De on www.krishnade.com

> **Promote your website address**
>
> Include your website address on all marketing material both online and offline from brochures to business cards, on other related websites, articles that you write for publications, etc. Aim to drive traffic to your website, particularly when the content is fresh and interesting.
>
> *Source: Krishna De, Internet marketing consultant*

3. LinkedIn

If you do not already have a profile up on LinkedIn, I advise you to go to www.linkedin.com and set one up. It is simple to register: you need your regular email address and a password for access. Then you set up a profile, with the assistance of a simple menu of choices. You can include as much detail as you want, and a photograph if you wish.

Science Fact

LinkedIn, which was established in 2003, is like a giant library of business connections. It has over 50 million members in more than two hundred countries worldwide. A new member joins LinkedIn approximately every second. Executives from all of the Fortune 500 companies are LinkedIn members.

It is not difficult to set up your profile on LinkedIn. Make sure that you complete your profile and keep it up to date. All the rules of communication apply here: your LinkedIn profile must reflect the values of your practice and be connected with the brand image you want to convey.

LinkedIn is important because people who want information about you will check your online profile. Clients, influencers and introducers all use LinkedIn to check out a person's details and pedigree.

I discovered the power of LinkedIn when conducting interviews for this book. One of the interviewees had a printout of my LinkedIn profile in front of him when I arrived. To be honest with you, I was surprised, because up until that moment, I had not realised just how important a reference point LinkedIn was. It made me wonder how many of the other people I interviewed had also looked up my credentials on LinkedIn.

LinkedIn is useful for developing profile and for establishing links with people you want to connect with. Krishna De tells the story of a contact she wanted to meet in a particular company. She had no introduction to this particular lady. She put the person's name into LinkedIn to discover whether any of her own connections were linked to this particular person. She discovered that a person she was acquainted with was linked to the lady in question. Krishna then wrote to her contact, requesting an introduction to the lady that she wanted to do business with. That is where LinkedIn can be better than any printed directory or networking event. If you are not there, you may miss out on opportunities.

Once you are up and running on LinkedIn, you can join international networking groups. For example, the Finance Accounting group has over 33,000 members; the Worldwide Management Consultants group has a membership of over 23,000; and the Professionals in Pharmaceutical and Biotech group has over 19,000 members. Closer to home, are groups connected to professional bodies such as Chartered Accountants Ireland, the Law Society of Ireland, Engineers Ireland, and so on.

4. Blogging

A 'blog' is an online journal that can be updated daily, weekly or even hourly if you wish.[78] Some companies have a website which contains the formal information about the company, and a blog which provides a more informal interaction. A number of smaller practitioners form their website around their blog.

There are a number of templates available online to help you set up a blog as part of a website. These include wordpress.com and blogger.com. A blog should contain relevant, interesting and stimulating content.

Look at other blogs before you start your own. The blogs that are most successful offer practical and useful, or very newsworthy, information. They have the added

Science Fact

advantage of drawing traffic to your website. To find out how to frame a blog, and what sort of content is relevant, you might like to begin by looking at:

Time magazine's top five most popular world blogs for 2009

- Talking Points Memo (www.talkingpointsmemo.com)
- The Huffington Post (www.huffingtonpost.com)
- Lifehacker (www.lifehacker.com)
- MetaFilter (www.metafilter.com)
- The Daily Dish by Andrew Sullivan (www.andrewsullivan.theatlantic.om)

---

78. Annmarie Hanlon. *QuickWin Marketing: Answers to Your Top 100 Marketing Questions* (Oak Tree Press, 2009)

A blog should not take up too much time, and yet it is important to keep your content fresh and topical.

You can use a blog to build exposure for your practice, to attract new clients and to establish yourself as an expert in your chosen market niche. The great thing is that you don't even have to have your own blog in order to do that.

The first step is to observe. Check out ongoing blogs as they relate to your practice. To find the right blogs for you to participate in, talk to people engaged in blogging and find out the more appropriate ones to engage in. Choose carefully, and find the blogs that make most sense for your business objectives, and ones that will give you an authoritative profile. Look out for blogs in your industry and related niches that are well linked to and respected. Technorati.com allows you to search for keywords and high-authority blogs.

If and when you establish your own blog, link it to your practice website. This has the dual role of drawing traffic to your site and increasing your profile as a thought leader.

When it comes to PR, blogging is becoming increasingly useful as a tool to reach a wide audience. A first step is to become a guest blogger either on someone else's website or as a participant in a discussion that is currently running. You can then link the blog to your own website. Journalists increasingly turn to blogs for newsworthy items. You can email a link to your blog to journalists, along with contact details if they need further information on a particular topic that you have discussed.

Twitter

Twitter is described as a 'micro blog'. Twitter asks one question: 'What are you doing?' Answers must be under 140 characters in length and can be sent via mobile texting, instant message, or the Web.[79] There are over 200 million people 'tweeting' worldwide, and this number is growing fast. In June 2009, there were 50,000 'tweeters' in Ireland, and this figure is increasing exponentially.[80]

---

79. www.twitter.com
80. *Sunday Business Post,* Agenda, 5 July 2009

Applied Science

Twitter has had some exceptional publicity. Take, for example, this excerpt from a Fox News bulletin in the United States:

Twitter links Iran protesters to the outside world

It was presidential election time in Iran – June 2009 – and protesters disputed the results. The authorities shut down text messaging, blocked Facebook and YouTube and cut off the BBC Persian language service – but they forgot about Twitter.[81]

The only way that the Western World could get information on the escalating violence in Tehran was via Twitter, and the White House asked Twitter's engineers not to take Twitter down for scheduled maintenance because the updates and photo images from Iran were too important.

Source: Fox News, 16 June 2009

Micro-blogging sites such as Twitter are ideal for celebrities who are building national or international profiles. Stephen Fry is one of the world's most prolific tweeters, with over a million followers. He made an announcement in 2009 that he was suspending his tweeting because he was addicted to it and it was taking up too much of his time.

While there is no doubt that Twitter is a powerful networking tool, micro-blogging takes up valuable time. Unless you are certain that your audience are ardent tweeters, it is probably not a priority for your practice. Statistics indicate that only 40 percent of Twitter accounts are maintained.

Check with your clients and your target audience. Is Twitter an important communication tool for them? Is it a way for you to connect with them? Is it a way to generate a profile for your practice? If so, tweet away. If not, tweet off and use your time elsewhere.

Science Fact

5. YouTube

YouTube is possibly the online tool with the most business potential in the next decade. YouTube was established in 2005 and now has 67.5 million unique users in the United States. Basically a Google-type search facility for videos, it has a myriad of personal and business uses.

---

81. Fox News website: www.foxnews.com/story/0,2933,526403,00.html

Creating videos has become much more cost-effective in recent years because of the increasing sophistication of home-video equipment. Videos can be recorded using iPods, mobile phones, iPhones and handycams, and these videos can be uploaded to YouTube in minutes.

If you decide to video a conference or seminar, or a training session, or a product demonstration, then YouTube is an ideal way to publicise it. Not everyone who is invited to an event can attend, so access to the podcast afterwards becomes a positive aspect of client service. The podcast can also be downloaded by key influencers, prospective clients and journalists when it suits them. This is a great way to make limited resources go further, to create differentiation, to increase the profile of your organisation, and to differentiate your business in your niche.

Mason Hayes and Curran Solicitors held a seminar on the subject of 'Fostering Entrepreneurship: Where to from here?' They invited leading entrepreneurs, academics and lobby groups to speak on the topic before an audience. The event was recorded and subsequently edited into a series of online videos that can be accessed through the Mason Hayes and Curran website.

Case study 5: An example of the power of digital media

At the Cannes Lions International Advertising Festival, one marketing campaign won more prestigious prizes than any other. This one campaign won a Grand Prix in the PR, direct marketing and cyber marketing categories. The awards have been around for fifty years; there were 22,000 entries this year, and no one campaign ever dominated three major categories.

You would imagine that the successful campaign was run by a major multinational with an enormous budget and a huge marketing team, but it wasn't. The winning campaign was run by a small tourism board promoting a little-known island off the Great Barrier Reef.[82] The marketing campaign is: 'The Best Job in the World'. In essence a worldwide recruitment campaign, the task was to recruit a caretaker for Hamilton Island, Queensland, Australia on a six month contract.

---

82. Rohit Bhargava, *Fast Company: 6 Lessons from the Best Marketing Campaign Ever*

It has been described as 'viral-marketing genius'. Why? Well, the campaign used the internet and social media – blogs, Facebook and Twitter – to attract the world's attention.

The results were startling: 34,000 video entries were posted on YouTube by people who talked about how much they liked Queensland, submitted from 200 countries. There were seven million hits to their website and 500,000 votes, leading to the eventual winner, British man Ben Southall, being chosen.[82]

Source: Fast Company: 6 Lessons from the Best Marketing Campaign Ever, by Rohit Bhargava

Science Facts

What lessons can professional practices learn from this campaign and its success?

- **The power of digital media.** We have reached a point where no one can afford to ignore social media as a part of an integrated marketing communications plan.

- **The future has arrived.** Digital media is not a part of our future; it is part of our present. As the figures tell us, millions of people worldwide are tuned in to social media sites such as LinkedIn, Facebook and Twitter.

- **Content creators are clients too.** A good proportion of your clients may be actively engaged with digital media and networking on the Web. It is worth finding out how your clients engage with social media.

- **Creativity doesn't have to cost a fortune.** As the story of the Queensland caretaker tells you, being creative on the Web does not necessarily cost a lot of money. You can use digital media to great effect to create an interesting brand for your practice. Make sure your content is good quality, that it tells an interesting story, and that people will want to become involved with you at some level.

- **Digital media is instantaneous.** Today, news travels faster by digital media than it does by any other medium – because it is instantaneous. The benefits for you are that you can communicate with a wide range of people both domestically and internationally in a matter of seconds.

---

82. Rohit Bhargava, *Fast Company: 6 Lessons from the Best Marketing Campaign Ever*

Part IV **Collaborate**

Work with others to gain new client introductions

16. Collaborate: The 5 Cs of Collaboration

Colleagues

Clients

Community

Collaborators

Competitors

Collaborate:
The Five Cs of Collaboration

16

'No one can whistle a symphony.
It takes a whole orchestra to play it.'

Dr Halford Luccock, Yale Divinity School

Collaboration is all about professionals working in conjunction with the wider community to promote solutions to clients. The recent economic decline has brought collaboration back into vogue, and it is widely talked about as a strategic way forward for organisations of all types and sizes.

Collaboration brings us back to community values and teamwork. It can be the most rewarding and stimulating part of your role because success ultimately comes from working as part of a team.

At a practical level, you probably have approximately 1,600 billable hours per annum at your disposal. A proportion of those hours must be given over to non-billable time so that you can engage in business development, networking and relationship-building. The most cost-effective way of using those hours is to collaborate and work as a team to develop your contacts and your public profile.

Why operate in isolation when you can collaborate with like-minded people who see the benefits of what you offer, can introduce you to the right people, and are happy to share ideas and opportunities?

Figure 30. The Five Cs of collaboration

1. Colleagues

2. Clients

3. Community

4. Collaborators

5. Competitors

1. Collaborating with colleagues

Your colleagues may be your employees, your peers or your boss, or a mix of all three. Collaborating with them to achieve your mission and objectives makes sense at every level. It is vital that all your associates share a common goal.

At one level, having everyone work together to achieve a big, audacious goal is exciting, motivating and powerful. When a team of colleagues is involved in planning, generating new ideas and even sharing the day-to-day running of a practice, there tend to be greater levels of motivation, commitment and trust. It has been said that teamwork divides the tasks and multiplies the success.

This chapter is not a study in employee motivation, which is beyond the scope of this book. However, it is worth remembering that tougher times can bring a greater team focus. This is important on two counts: most professionals are looking more closely at the value their employees bring to the practice, and employees are more willing to adapt their work practices to ensure that they deliver greater results for the firm they work with. This is a time to choose the best collaborators around you, the ones who are willing to co-operate, innovate and go the extra mile to deliver for clients.

My research for **Client Science** showed that competition among partners in some firms could sometimes divert important time and attention away from the critical aspect of the business: clients. This is an age-old challenge for firms, and it will never be easily resolved. However, within your sphere of influence, you can make a difference by creating an open and challenging atmosphere. Involve colleagues as much as possible in the future direction of your practice and collaborate with them to create a vision that they can all share with you.

Your colleagues provide many of the skills and input required to implement new ideas, visions and strategies. Involving employees in the future of your organisation is vital particularly during an economic downturn, when there may be concerns about redundancy or, more pertinently, a lack of work at the practice:

- Employees can provide valuable insight

- They need to be bought in from an early stage to mitigate their concerns

- If there is cause for concern, they should be close enough to the centre to understand the issues involved and to make decisions for themselves about their future.

Applied Science

The converse of collaboration is resistance. This can be difficult and time-consuming to deal with, particularly if you have to make substantial changes to your organisation in order for it to be sustainable for the future.

Here are five useful considerations when it comes to collaborating with colleagues:

- **Don't assume that you know everything.** Never make assumptions about how your colleagues, clients or associates will react to your business, a promotion or a promise.

- **Pilot new initiatives and get employee feedback.** Once a new initiative or campaign is out in the market, it cannot be taken back. So be conscious of the impact that any new initiatives may have on your people and your clients. If you release a new idea on a pilot or test basis, then you will have the opportunity to gather feedback and collaborate on refining it, if this is required.

- **Provide advance notice on communications.** There are situations that I have come across where, through advertising or public announcements, clients know about a new initiative before employees. This scenario almost always creates a negative impression both on employees, who are unable to respond to queries, and on clients, who are confused by an inadequate response to their queries. Make your employees and those in your wider sphere of influence aware of any communication that may generate a response so that they can respond to queries effectively and deliver for you.

- **Sense check and review.** Colleagues will often be the first to be aware of how systems, initiatives or products are not delivering as effectively as they should. Carefully measure the ongoing success of your initiatives and improvements. Do sense checks with colleagues, clients and collaborators to ensure that you are achieving your desired results.

- **Deal positively and immediately with client complaints.** Set up a complaints log, a complaints-handling process and a professional approach to client redress. Create an environment where employees can report client complaints at the highest levels. Deal with those complaints until they are completely resolved. Don't leave disgruntled clients to go elsewhere before you respond.

2. Client collaboration is a two-way flow

Science Fact The very best service providers, in any industry, sit down with clients at the end of a project or transaction and ask 'How was it for you?' This may be referred to as a review meeting, a debrief or a close-out session. In effect, this is one of your most critical client collaboration meetings.

Collaboration with clients is one of the best ways to improve your competitiveness and to identify new services and new ways to deliver your services.[83]

Clients experience your service and your work first hand, and become intimately aware of the positive and negative aspects of doing business with you.

It is worth noting that the quality of work might not be the same as the quality of your service. Speak to clients about their perception of both. Did the work satisfy their needs? Did the quality of the service and how the work was delivered meet their expectations? These opportunities for feedback should not be ignored: they are extremely valuable.

Even in these debrief meetings, many professionals do not go far enough in asking for suggestions for improvement. Feedback is useful, and clients are usually pleased

---

83. David Maister, *Managing the Professional Services Firm* (Simon & Schuster UK, 2003)

to provide it. This is an opportunity for you to discuss improvements and is worth spending time on. Seek suggestions for positive change. The people who experience the service are usually the ones with the best ideas for improvements.

What better collaboration than one that results in positive comments? Record the positive remarks that people make about your service, your team, and the way in which your expertise has benefited them. This feedback is good for your organisation; it can be incorporated into your sales pitch and your marketing material.

Ask your client if you can use their positive recommendation in your client testimonials, on your website and as part of presentations to prospective clients. Also, feed back the positive commentary to employees and all members of the team who serviced the client – including those less directly involved, such as, for example, receptionists, the IT team, etc. Sounds all too much? These days, we all need the boost; it's worth a few blushes.

In previous chapters, I talked about how existing clients are often ignored in favour of business development initiatives to find new clients. Firms and practices often believe that existing clients don't need further attention or courting – but they do. An existing client is less expensive to service, is already familiar with your systems, and is **Applied Science** known to you and your team. How do you collaborate with clients to further enhance the relationship and get mutual value? Reciprocity is important at this juncture: you both have to benefit.

- **Become a client of your client.** This is not always possible, but if it is, you can become as valued a client to them as they are to you. There's no better mutuality than that.

- **Share contacts and introductions.** Ask your clients for introductions to new business, if they are satisfied with your service. Most clients are amenable, but are seldom asked for introductions.

- **Training.** Are there opportunities to learn from each other? Share skills wherever possible, and work together to get the best from your team.

- **Client testimonials.** Produce a jointly branded document, podcast, webpage or web video on how you work together. Often, testimonials are done from one perspective – a client commenting on the great work done by the professional services firm. However, a truly effective client testimonial willl talk about the excellence of both the client and the professional.

- **Arrange joint seminars or presentations.** This works particularly well at business-to-business level, where the respective skills of the client and the professional complement each other and can be used for presentation purposes.

Science Fact

Clients and introductions

Over 80 percent of clients are never asked for introductions to other clients. The vast majority of clients would be delighted to provide introductions to prospective clients for the professionals that did a good job for them.[84] That's a lot of business that has never been asked for.

Most professionals traditionally relied on word-of-mouth introductions to their practices. Clients referred to your practice tend to be more loyal and less expensive than those who come from any other source. Introductions from associates and other clients, which are built on trust, rapport and competence, mean that you get clients who, when they walk through your door, have already decided that they want your expertise.[85]

The message is that it is all right to ask clients, for whom you have done a good job and from whom you have obtained good feedback, for names of people who they believe would also make suitable clients for you.

Science Fact

It is time for us to overcome our reticence about asking for business. In modern business, it is expected that you will ask for introductions and to be recommended. The client may not always think of it unless you do.

3. Community

Every business takes a position in the marketplace. It's called reputation. Reputation depends on how highly regarded your business is by clients, the community and other influencers. Reputation also encompasses what your business is known for, how your practice is described in relation to competitors, and, most importantly, how your practice is positioned in the minds of existing and potential clients.

---

84. C Mark Lloydbottom and David W. Cottle, *Clients4life* (Institute of Chartered Accountants of Scotland, 2008)
85. Mark Powers and Shawn McNalis, *How Good Attorneys Become Great Rainmakers* (Independently published, 2009)

What part do you want to play in your community? How do you want to measure up against your competitors in your local environment? How would you like people in close proximity to you to describe your business? To establish a reputation in your community, you not only serve it, you become involved with it – in fact, become a key participant in it.

One of the critical things about collaboration at community level is that it is mutually beneficial and interdependent. A focus on community interaction has enormous benefits for those who are prepared to give time and participate. It is not just about business; it is about relationships.

Look around you. Who are the influencers in your community that can help you profile your service locally and spread the word about what you do? Look beyond the obvious and think about how you can really make community a worthwhile investment for your practice.

The contacts that you seek include:

- **Key business and professional people.** There are usually a small number of people who practically run the local area. It is useful to be acquainted with the people who know and understand the local dynamics and the key players.

- **Colleges and schools.** Community-based educational facilities can provide excellent opportunities for you to work with students and lecturers.

- **Local business organisations.** Chambers and other business promotion organisations are generally very supportive of all types of business, and they can open doors to new opportunities for you.

- **Local sports clubs and entertainment organisations.** The people you enjoy playing sports and socialising with can become part of your collaborative network.

- **Online professional networks.** These networks, such as LinkedIn, are designed to create networking communities via the Internet. Set up your own profile and invite people you know to associate with you.

- **Political representatives.** Get to know your local politicians: they tend to have a wide range of contacts and an influential network behind them.

- **Government-backed business agencies.** These agencies, such as the Enterprise Boards, FÁS and business incubation centres tend to have good information resources on the business community.

This is not an exhaustive list. There are many other key people and organisations who will gladly open up opportunities for you to network within the territory that you have earmarked for your business development plans.

Do business in your local community

Applied Science How can you expect to be successful in setting out your own stall in your local community if you don't get do business with the people around you?

Seán, a business banker, talks about how you cannot do business successfully in a local community unless you are prepared to be involved with that community: 'You shop in the local shops, your children attend the local schools and you attend and participate in the local events.'

When it comes to sourcing supplies, employing people, and locating your premises, consider the implications from a local perspective. Loyalty begins at home.

Get involved in corporate social responsibility (CSR)

CSR is a broad term that covers everything from business ethics to environmental awareness and involvement with charity.

Charity

Unfortunately, in tough times, charity organisations often experience a significant reduction in the amount of funds they can raise. Some businesses and practices that have recognised this have diverted funding away from client and staff entertainment, and towards involvement with charity. There are ways to do this sensitively and inclusively, so that colleagues and clients can become involved in charity events and projects.

Many annual Christmas lunches include fund-raising for selected charities as part of the event. There are a number of major dinners, auctions, fashion shows and other events held annually in aid of charities.

National charities. A good example of a national charity event, and how you might get involved, is the Welcome Home Wexford Cycle, in aid of the Peter McVerry Trust, where more than 400 professionals cycle from Dublin to Wexford annually to raise funds for homeless young people. The camaraderie that you experience from events like this cycle is tremendous. These events build great bonds of friendship as well as raise valuable money for charity.

International charities. A number of business professionals in Ireland have worked hard abroad to make a difference to people in dire straits. Here is just one example of how it works.

When **Educo**, the Irish-registered charity set up to educate disadvantaged children, wanted to raise funds, they dreamed up a truly memorable collaboration initiative. Educo's aim is to open a school each year in India; they have opened schools in Sahar slum, Mumbai; Vasai; and Kolkata.

Educo approached Dublin-based portrait photographer Shane McCarthy, who has photographed Bono, Cate Blanchett, Brian O'Driscoll and a host of other celebrities. They wanted a top photographer to travel to India to capture the work of Educo for fund-raising purposes.

The result is an impressive collection of photographs including: shoeless children giggling against a wall; a child labourer transporting bricks on his head; two little girls picking their way through the Mumbai slums to school, and many others. The photographs were auctioned successfully to raise funds for the Educo charity organisation.

Environmental awareness. The green energy and environmental awareness sector has become big business. It is estimated that this segment of the market was worth over €500 billion by the end of 2009. Forfás estimate that the Irish market is worth over €2.8 billion. The sub-sectors that are considered to have the greatest potential are: renewable energies; efficient energy use and management (including eco-construction); waste management, recovery and recycling; water and wastewater treatment; and environmental consultancy and services.

So consider the environment as a sector for your practice from two perspectives:

- **Business development.** This is a growth sector worth billions. What are the opportunities for you?

- **Practice awareness.** This is a now considered to be a basic and essential part of your community involvement, both locally and globally. Using energy as efficiently as possible, using recycled paper and recycling waste are the obvious things, and we should all be doing them as a matter of course.

The interesting thing about collaboration is that it broadens your skills set. Community collaboration almost always challenges a person or an organisation to dig deeper to find new or untested capability. In my experience, the added benefit of collaboration is that it promotes development at personal and at practical level and it is rewarding.

4. Collaborators

Collaborators are people who can bring expertise and opportunities to your practice; they come in many forms. Look around you and identify the sort of people who can help you achieve your objectives and be broadminded when it comes to choosing collaborators. These might include:

Retired people who once practised the same profession as you. They may still have the inside track on business, potential business and relevant issues and opportunities. Many of those who have retired and 'seen it all' retain the business acumen and wealth of experience that made them successful.

New non-executive directors. You may seek to bring diverse expertise onto your board, to help you build your business, or so that you can benefit from a different type of experience. Banks invite entrepreneurs, academics and industry leaders onto their boards, for example. People who are highly successful in their own sectors can bring tremendous insight and knowledge to the boardroom table.

Consultants. It is often cheaper to outsource certain functions to external consultants who can provide expertise in areas such as HR, marketing, strategy and PR, systems and technology.

Young people. Young people can bring a valuable approach to problem-solving. They are very often technologically savvy, have fresh ideas and are in tune with what is in vogue. Involve young graduates in your brainstorming sessions. Give them the opportunity to express themselves. Raw talent can bring some interesting thinking to your practice.

Seek out a diverse and interesting range of collaborators that you can pick up the phone to when you need them. The more input you have from people, the more informed your thinking will be, and the more confident you will be in making necessary changes to your practice – to win in the marketplace.

5. Co-operative competitors

There are times when it is worth thinking about how and where you might collaborate with competitors. Doctors who form a clinic together are collaborating competitors. Solicitors jointly establishing a legal firm are also collaborating competitors. There are many advantages to collaborating with competitors. You learn more, you gain greater understanding of your market, and you build your network. (Collaboration should always happen, of course, in compliance with any relevant competition laws. I am not suggesting collusion or the creation of cartels.)

Stockbrokers for financial stability: A collective response on Ireland

In April 2009, three stockbroking firms got together in response to a looming economic meltdown to present their joint report on how to improve the country's financial situation. The firms were Davy Stockbrokers, Goodbody Stockbrokers and NCB.

The report they produced was called *Charting the Course to Irish Economic and Financial Stability*. It was a compendium of their collective advice and recommendations on how to improve Ireland's finances. The team began by saying:

- The issues facing the Irish economy and Irish society have never been more challenging, and more than ever a collective response is required.
- We, Ireland's three largest stockbrokers, have put aside our competitive instincts to make a common proposal for addressing our national difficulties.

Their report is a clear illustration of how competitive collaboration can be a force for good, and can contribute positively. As a reputation-building exercise, the initiative demonstrates maturity, forward-thinking and openness.

Global competitors

A number of Irish professional firms collaborate with similar firms abroad, to great effect. Most of the international competitive collaborators aren't actually competing in the Irish market; this makes the collaboration particularly useful.

Professionals from Irish firms go out into the international markets specifically to make contact with their counterparts in organisations in America, Europe and, more recently, Asia. The collaborative agreements that are made between the international and Irish organisations mean that introductions, or elements of business that need to be conducted through Ireland, are referred by the counterparty abroad to the link firm in Ireland; the reverse is also the case.

There are established groups formed between firms internationally where each country is represented by one participating practice and introductions relating to those countries are passed to the representative firm. The groups tend to be tight-knit, and many, particularly in the legal sector, are closed to new entrants – having been established many years ago. However, there are always opportunities for you to establish your own groups, to link with firms abroad that could potentially have business with Ireland and to forge relationships with international competitors.

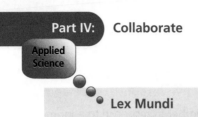

Lex Mundi

Lex Mundi is an international group of law firms. The group has a membership of more than 21,000 lawyers in 160 member firms, with more than 560 offices in 100 countries.

Members are prominent local law firms recognised for the breadth and depth of their legal expertise, their reputations in their jurisdictions, and the quality of their client service.

As the exclusive representative for its jurisdiction, each member firm must provide the full range of legal services required by commercial clients and must be a leader in the use of technology as well as in law firm management.

The benefits of collaborating with competitors

LinkedIn, the online business networking service I discussed in the last chapter, makes collaboration with competitors a normal part of life. There are hundreds of groups that you can join online in order to discuss new ideas and share information with people working in your field either nationally or worldwide.

Competitor collaboration also takes place at industry conferences, which are an interesting way to learn about new developments and trade experiences with people operating in the same field as you.

A form of competitor collaboration is the proliferation of industry training programmes that bring people from firms and practices together for learning purposes. Encourage your team to take advantage of these opportunities where you can: they are a great way to develop contacts and broaden your sphere of thinking.

The great benefits of competitor collaboration include:

- Sharing ideas
- Learning about new developments in technology, specialist training and skills
- Accessing group training and broadening your competency base
- Receiving introductions to new clients
- Sharing best practice
- Trading information on operating systems and service experience
- Accessing white papers and industry insights
- Learning about new markets, new segments and new trends

Here are ten ways to widen your network

I haven't included the typical ones, like attending conferences, joining LinkedIn and joining clubs. They have been covered already.

- **Get to know everyone who attends client meetings.** How often have you walked away from a client meeting without getting to know the non-core people who attended with your main contact? Introduce yourself, exchange cards and establish a rapport. They may be useful to you.[86]

- **Arrange your own networking events.** Invite clients, their associates and other local influencers to an event at your office. As the host, everyone who attends is open to you. You can ask those you invite to bring a contact – which will naturally widen your network.

- **Become a key speaker.** Make yourself available as a thought leadership speaker and give talks as an expert to groups of potential clients.

- **Ask clients for introductions.** Though already suggested it is worth repeating. Clients don't usually mind.

- **Chat with people you meet.** On planes, on trains, in queues, at events.

- **Work your suppliers.** You pay them, so raise the possibility of reciprocal arrangements – wherever this is appropriate. Make sure to provide them with information about what you do and look for introductions to the decision-makers in their wider organisation.

- **Keep family and friends informed.** We're not talking pyramid selling here. If you don't do so already, make sure that your family and friends are informed about the sort of professional work you do, so that they can recommend you, where the opportunity comes up.

- **Use your banker, your accountant, your solicitor.** It's amazing how well connected these people are. Make sure that your financial and legal people understand the business you are in. They can't recommend you exclusively, but they can add you to their list of people to talk to. Their clients often ask them for recommendations.

---

86. Ford Harding. *Rain Making* (Adams Business, 2008)

- **Invite people for coffee.** I'm not a fan of cold-calling. You probably aren't either. I have done it, though, and some of those calls resulted in productive meetings. The best advice I ever got about cold-calling was to invite people for coffee. So whether you decide to knock on the door of a target client in your locality, or pick up the phone to someone you have on your target list – offer to buy them a cup of coffee. This is so much more inviting than a cold meeting.

- **Hold a supper club evening.** Londoners use this as a way to draw together an eclectic mix of people. The supper club is a completely informal and relaxed dinner – at an exclusive venue. Invite a mix of prospective clients for a relaxed networking evening, and place the priority on excellent food and drink. Some invitations are hard to refuse.

Part V   Calculate

Measure the success of your marketing initiatives

17. Calculate: Five tools to measure marketing success

Calculate:
Five tools to measure marketing success

17

> '*Life is filled with truly unfathomable potential . . .
> in most cases, our so-called limitations are nothing
> more than our own decision to limit ourselves.*'

Daisaku Ikeda, Buddhist leader

At this point, we've come full circle in the bid to achieve the big, audacious goal set out in **Chapter 1**. It's time to measure the success of your marketing and sales activity and to decide which of these initiatives have produced the best results for your organisation.

We began by setting objectives, deciding who to target and where to position a practice to maximise your competitive edge. Step two is about creating a value proposition to support those objectives, and step three is about communicating the proposition to the market. In Part Four, we discussed the power of collaboration in marketing a practice. The fifth step is now to measure the success of the various initiatives that make up your marketing plan.

The role of marketing is to measure and anticipate the needs and requirements of a group of clients and to respond with a flow of need-satisfying goods and services. This allows you to target the customer groups whose needs are most consistent with your resources and capabilities, and to develop products and services that meet the needs of the target market better than your competitors.

Marketing is a not an exact science: much of it is about trying out new ideas to see which ones will produce results. There are so many variables involved, from markets and economies, to trends and new developments, through to competition. One thing I can guarantee is that a practice that uses marketing will fare better than one that does not. If you measure client satisfaction, you are more likely to understand and do something to improve your ratings. If you have a sales pipeline in place, you are more likely to set targets for new-client acquisition. If you engage in PR, you are more likely to improve your reputation locally. Likewise, measuring profitability helps you focus on how to be more profitable.

There are five ways to measure the success of marketing:

Figure 31. Five tools to measure the marketing success

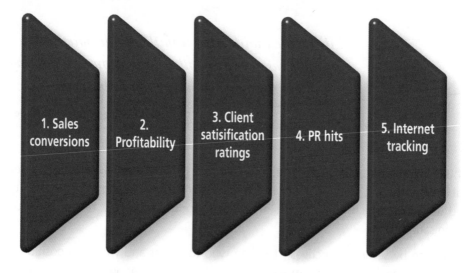

1. Sales conversions
2. Profitability
3. Client satisification ratings
4. PR hits
5. Internet tracking

1. Sales conversions

In **Chapter 3**, we discussed the idea of a sales pipeline. This can be a simple spreadsheet that allows you to track your sales activity, from when they are target names, to when you send them an initial proposal and pricing, right through to when they confirm that they will actually become your client. The sales pipeline spreadsheet is a simple but effective document to help monitor sales activity. Your overall sales success is measured by the number of conversions that you have. Conversions are the target names that become actual paying clients.

How many conversions you should have depends very much on the type of practice that you run. For some practices, like engineering or architecture, one major client may be enough to sustain the business for a period of time; for others, like banks, doctors and accountants, a much higher volume of conversions is necessary.

New clients cannot be measured in isolation. For each quarter, keep a record of the number of clients that no longer do business with you.

Your most important measurement figure is your net clients figure:

Figure 32. Net clients analysis

Quarter 1	Quarter 2	Quarter 2	Client 2
Total number of clients	Client conversions	Clients lost	Net Clients
102	4	4	102

As the table above illustrates, the sales effort has to work in tandem with client retention in order to build your business.

Here are five tips to help you measure your sales activity:

- Actively manage your prospects using your sales pipeline
- Keep track of the sources that introduce new clients to you, and regularly acknowledge their input to your business
- Learn from your wins and losses as you pitch for business
- Keep track of your success rates
- Communicate your successes with other members of your practice, and celebrate wins.

Measure the use of your time if you are a sole trader, and that of your team if you are in partnership. Out of an average of 1,600 billing hours a year, you may spend up to 300 on sales and business development. This represents a significant cost to you and your practice. Carefully measure the results that you get from those 300 hours, and focus on the activity that can maximise your conversions.

It can be acceptable to lose clients if this is intentional and they are low-value and high-input – and therefore unprofitable. Remember, though, that it costs up to six times as much to recruit a client as it does to retain an existing one.

2. Profitability

There is an old saying in the accountancy profession: turnover is vanity, profit is sanity, and cash is reality. Typically, it is profitability that is most important for a practice, but always keep in mind that getting paid – or, more precisely, cash receipts – is a key measure of the success of your practice and, in the current climate, very important to its survival.

In **Chapter 4**, I talked about Harvard professor Robert Kaplan's 'Whale Curve', and about how up to 300 percent of profitability can be lost when it costs more to serve clients than you can bill them. You will know that your marketing is working if you have moved a significant proportion of clients from the 'C' or 'D' to 'A' or 'B' category or, alternatively, if you have divested 'E' clients in a way that hasn't damaged the fabric of your business.

Through diversification of product streams, added value and a focus on cross-selling, you will aim to bring a number of your clients from the break-even level to the highly profitable 'A' or 'B' zone.

The profitability of your client is measured by:

- fee income
- timeliness of payment, if at all
- high or low maintenance required
- number of introductions or referrals received from the client for new business
- overall loyalty and satisfaction with your services.

All of these elements can be measured in some form. Fee income is probably the simplest form of measurement.

The level of maintenance required is more subjective and may be judged by the number and duration of phone calls, presentation of information by the client, and general attitude. On your sales pipeline, you can easily record the number of referrals that you receive from each of your clients for new business. Satisfaction can be recorded as part of the overall client interface, and through a satisfaction survey.

Traditionally, the focus has been on the short-term transactional value of the client, but the really successful professionals and firms that I interviewed tended to focus more on long-term value. Compute the lifetime value of a client, and the income levels will astound you. Lifetime customer value is the total value of revenue that can be produced by a client over time. Take into consideration the probable introductions to new clients that you will receive from a long-term client, and you begin to see the need for retention and loyalty programmes.

Another way to measure the value of a client is to calculate how many products or services each client takes up. If your clients currently average two to three products each, aim to increase that figure to four. Again, this will significantly contribute to your bottom line, and to the chances of you retaining your clients for the long term.

3. Client satisfaction ratings

The ultimate satisfaction of the client depends on whether the service lives up to expectations and delivers the anticipated benefits. It is not enough to get the work; you have to live up to the client's expectations. In **Chapter 7**, we discussed how you can measure client satisfaction. Aim to measure how satisfied your clients are with your service at least once every eighteen months.

Use the same rating scales each time so that you can compare results.

Aim for over 95 percent in your client satisfaction ratings. Clients expect to be entirely satisfied with the service that you offer. Those that experience even 5 percent dissatisfaction are at risk of finding services elsewhere.

4. PR 'hits'

When you send out a press release to a number of publications, it is not always easy to find out which paper or magazine actually ran with your story. Different publications choose different dates to print an article on a particular topic. At the same time, you have to know what publicity you received in order to measure the success of your PR campaign, and to help you decide which topics carry more weight with the media over time.

Another important aspect of measuring PR is the value of an article run by a paper free-of-charge. When you compare the cost for placement of an advertisement of a similar size to a free PR story, you soon get the measure of the value of your PR campaign.

To track your stories, or references to your firm in the print media, there are a number of media-monitoring agencies offering their services. Some agencies can provide you with an online facility to track the publicity for your practice on a daily basis. Others can supply press clippings and transcripts of radio or television interviews. You can take up the media-monitoring service as you need it; costs vary depending on the amount of tracking that is required, and the length of time that tracking is carried out.

A free service from Google, Google Alerts, allows you to monitor news updates, Web pages and interactive information for mention of specific names or terms. Google then alerts you by email if it comes across a result that matches your specified request.

Google Alerts is useful to monitor mention of your practice name, or information on a specific topic, or for information on competitors.

5. Internet tracking

In **Chapter 15**, we looked at digital marketing and cloud computing, and how modern marketing requires that you have a well-developed website, a blog and a LinkedIn profile. There are two broad areas of measurement for website marketing. The first is Search Engine Optimisation (SEO), which helps place your website ahead of those of your competitors when people input a request for information into a search engine (the most commonly used of which is Google). Google's goal is to 'return highly relevant results for every query'; it works on the basis of a mathematical algorithm that involves over 200 factors. This algorithm changes frequently; as a result, search engine optimisation companies have to work very hard to keep up.[87] The second aspect of website measurement is the tracking feature. It is now possible to track traffic on your website, to discover which pages people tend to navigate to most.

There are many companies that promise to provide you with SEO, and you should get references from their existing clients before you spend money on it. SEO is an area that has become increasingly sophisticated. Once upon a time, it involved liberally spreading the keywords that clients most use through your website information. Now, a search engine uses much more forensic detail to identify the best websites.

A search engine will place a website high on the list for the following five reasons:

- The website has been submitted to search engines.

- The site is search-engine friendly. This includes having uncomplicated names for website pages and layout, not too many images, and not too much text.

- The website is regularly updated with relevant and useful content for visitors, such as latest news, information polls and latest market updates. Your blog is particularly useful here, to keep content up to date and interactive.

- The more popular a website is, the more likely it is to be picked up by a search engine. One of the criteria for high placement of a site by a search engine is the amount of traffic it already attracts.

---

87. Annmarie Hanlon, *QuickWin Marketing: Answers to Your Top 100 Marketing Questions* (Oak Tree Press, 2009)

- If other websites contain links to your website, you are more likely to attract the attention of a search engine.

You can attract more hits to your website by emailing people with information containing links to your site. The link might be to a newsletter, an update or a members' section on your website. Part of your collaboration strategy with non-competing organisations in your community is to place a link to your website on other websites, and in return to place their link on yours. Also, provide information about your website as part of your email address, business cards, brochures, client testimonials and pitch books, and suggest verbally to people that they check out your website.

To measure hits to your website, you can do a number of things. First, within your content management system, ensure that there is a traffic tracking and reporting system so that you can observe the volume of traffic to your site, and to particular pages of your site.

You may offer regular clients more in-depth information in a members' section of your site. The number of members you attract each quarter is a useful measurement. You may also want people to register for certain events, seminars or white papers online; again, the response rate can be easily measured. Finally, make sure that there is a 'Contact Us' form to help you capture details of prospective clients.

In conclusion

It seems appropriate, as I conclude this book, to revisit Asia. One of the most striking features that I came across was the Longji – Dragon's Backbone - Rice Terraces in Southern China. The rice terraces are ingeniously built into steep hillsides, as high as 880 metres, in order to make the best use of the scarce arable land and water resources in the mountainous region.

These remarkable paddy fields have been cleverly constructed over hundreds of years and they are built with a perfect balance of understanding, innovation and nurturing. In the beginning, the Chinese saw an enormous challenge: how to harness the mountain waters to create paddy fields in an area where flat plains were scarce. Creativity and vision led the people to etch rice terraces into the steep hills and they constantly monitored and nurtured the terraces to ensure that they maintained the perfect balance of water needed to produce rice.

You too must find a good balance in building your practice, giving due consideration to today's challenging market conditions and at the same time creating a successful and robust business model for the future. The **Five C's** provides an ideal template to help you to win clients and develop your professional practice by encouraging you to:

- Pull together the information that you need to understand the challenges and identify the opportunities.

- Carefully consider how you manage your practice, your employees, your clients and your service offering to create an exemplary and profitable organisation.

- Communicate in a way that achieves success using a mix of traditional and modern communications techniques and to keep those around you informed of your progress, particularly your clients, community and employees.

- Collaborate widely to spread your message, and finally

- Continually monitor your progress by calculating the success of your initiatives and always seeking interesting ways to improve.

The Longji Rice Terraces do not function without understanding, innovation and nurturing. Similarly, your practice needs a constant balance of the Five C's – **Collate, Create, Communicate, Collaborate and Calculate** – to expand and grow continually.

Client Science gives you the tools for success and the rest is up to you. Good luck!

Appendix

The fifty-five professionals interviewed for this book

The fifty-five professionals who helped in the research for *Client Science*

1	Sinead Allen, Lavelle Coleman
2	Aidan Bodkin, Share Navigator
3	Anne Brady, Anne Brady McQuillans DFK
4	Kirsten Breen, Baker Tilly Ryan Glennon
5	Eddie Brown, Ulster Bank Invoice Finance
6	Angela Carr, living:room Architecture and Design
7	Brian Clarke, Brian Clarke & Associates
8	Maria Colgan, Bloxham Stockbrokers
9	Rosemary Collier, Forté International
10	Catherine Corcoran, Baker Tilly Ryan Glennon
11	Ted Corcoran, Leadership Consultant
12	Stephen Cox, Share Navigator
13	Krishna De, BizGrowthMedia
14	Robert Dix, Sopal / formerly KPMG
15	Tony Duffy, Commercial Finance Ireland
16	Rosemary Fagan, Lisney
17	John Fanning, Brand Consultant / formerly McConnells Advertising
18	Fiona Flynn, Sales Solutions
19	Maree Gallagher, Maree Gallagher Associates
20	Margaret Gilsenan, Boys and Girls Advertising
21	Eithne Harley, Mason Hayes & Curran
22	Brian Horgan, Ulster Bank
23	Ron Immink, smallbusinesscan.com
24	Tom Keane, Dalríada
25	Bertie Kelly, National College of Ireland
26	David Kelly, KendleBell and Capita
27	Derek Keogh, Anglo Irish Bank
28	Jimmy Kinahan, Engineers Ireland
29	Peter Killeen, Custom House Square Medical Centre

30	Eamonn Leahy, Leahy & Co
31	Ian Lucey, Lucey Technology
32	Tom Martin, Econiq
33	Lynda McCracken, Innovation Employment
34	Shane McCarthy, Photographer
35	Ciaran McGowan, Staff Balance
36	John McGrane, Ulster Bank
37	Neal Morrison, McInerney Saunders, Chartered Accountants
38	Jon Mulligan, Openplain
39	Cariona Neary, Neary Marketing & Communications
40	Ana Nelson, Bloxham Stockbrokers
41	Padhraig Nolan, Artisan Design
42	Laurence O'Brien, Deep Insight
43	Sheira O'Brien, Zenith
44	Claire O'Connor, O'Connor & Associates
45	Brian O'Kane, Oak Tree Press
46	Paul O'Neill, Chartered Accountant
47	Fionan O'Tierney, Chartered Accountant
48	Vincent Power, A&L Goodbody
49	Roddy Rowan, Genesis
50	Gerard McInerney , McInerney Saunders Chartered Accountants
51	Gerard Tannam, Islandbridge Brand Direction
52	Michael Torpey, Irish Life & Permanent
53	Sean Torpey, Ulster Bank
54	Liam Twohig, Baker Tilly Ryan Glennon
55	Seán Weafer, Seanweafer.com